MW00940345

To Jean.
Enjoy —
Carol

We Interrupt This Childhood to Bring You World War II

by

Carol Dickey Watson

Bloomington, IN Milton Keynes, UK

authorHOUSE®

AuthorHouse™
1663 Liberty Drive, Suite 200
Bloomington, IN 47403
www.authorhouse.com
Phone: 1-800-839-8640

AuthorHouse™ UK Ltd.
500 Avebury Boulevard
Central Milton Keynes, MK9 2BE
www.authorhouse.co.uk
Phone: 08001974150

First published by AuthorHouse 4/19/2007

ISBN: 978-1-4259-6208-1 (sc)

Printed in the United States of America
Bloomington, Indiana

This book is printed on acid-free paper.

Dedicated in memory

of

Jordan David Ellis

Firefighter, EMT,

Humanitarian

and my beloved grandson

The happiest moments of my
life have been the few which
I have passed at home in the
bosom of my family.
Thomas Jefferson

WHEN INNOCENCE ENDED

My brother had just turned three years old and I was nine when President Roosevelt made his famous Date of Infamy speech; neither of us was old enough to grasp what was causing the anxious, worried expressions on the faces of those we loved. We did know, however, that something was very wrong. When the entire family gathered closely around the Atwater-Kent radio and weighed each word being uttered, we realized it was time to be still; a task much easier for me than for my very active little brother.

I don't suppose we had ever heard the word "war" except when Uncle Collin had amused us by letting us try on a military cap he owned, or possibly when we had seen a movie about the subject. The word became more and more a part of our parents' conversations when Bubba was one year old and Germany marched into Poland. The only uniforms I had paid much attention to were the ones my uncles had worn as cadets at Schriener Institute, a military prep school in the Texas Hill country.

In a peaceful community such as ours real conflict was as foreign as the other side of the moon. It was an age of recovery from what our parents called "The Depression," though I didn't know what they meant by the term. Our family enjoyed the simple pleasures of life; important things like celebrating a birthday, making a freezer of fresh peach ice cream and going on picnics. The grown-ups worked hard throughout the week but, weekends were devoted to family outings church activities and discussions of civic affairs.

It took some major adjustments to become accustomed to the changes that were to take place after December 7, 1941. Our family rallied together to meet the various challenges. One by one, each member of our clan became involved in his or her own contributions to the war effort. Patriotism became a way of life; a oneness of purpose permeated every aspect of our lives in a way this nation had never experienced before. It was a sad age, a purposeful age, a confusing age, an historic age, a maturing age, a frightful age and a charitable age all rolled into one short period of history.

Our innocence then was the result of our small town environment, one isolated from the pressures of the city: unhurried, easy going and altruistic. The changes came quickly and continued at a numbing pace until at last the war was over. By then our whole little world had ceased to exist as it once was; never to return again.

In each of our lives are times we hold dear, not unlike the memories of those we have loved and lost to the inevitability of death. You may call it history, biography, remembrance or living in the past, but by whatever name it remains a personal treasure to be shared with those who succeed you.

I do not mourn the loss of these times for they are still with me. This book is a chronicle of a time that was and is no more; a time to be remembered; a heritage to be passed on to new generations; a gift of the past for those who now look only to the future.

In order to understand the changes, and their effects, we must pause long enough to discover how it was.

My Home Town

My home town of Crockett was a small Texas city of 5,000 souls who were aware of world events and the arts and such, but who derived much more pleasure from their small groups of acquaintances than they did from outside events. There is a beautifully lilting ring to the words,"my home town" whether they are uttered with New England inflections, Southern drawls or Southwestern twangs, for these three single syllable words recall memories all of us cherish.

Our downtown featured drug stores owned by Mr. Chamberlain, Mr. Van Pelt, Mr. Goolsby, Mr. Bishop and Mr. Julian. There were two weekly newspapers, The Crockett Democrat and The Crockett Courier. The McCarty, McConnell, Shivers, Oziers and Traylor families all owned all general merchandise stores where one could buy work boots, sewing notions, piece goods, ready-made clothing, linens and a little of most anything else one might want in soft goods. The variety stores, Duke and Ayres, Spidle's Five and Dime and Perry Brothers held awesome attractions especially for the kids because they had candy, fresh popcorn, fireworks (at Christmas), coloring books, school supplies and, of course, our favorite comic books. Ladies did their grocery shopping at a number of stores; Caprielian Brothers, R. L. Shivers General Merchandise. Bennett's Grocery, Morrow's Food Market and Brookshire Brothers.

On the east end of the business area was the Ritz Theater, where first run movies were shown , while on the west side of the courthouse square was the Texas Theater, specializing in cowboy shows and featuring the 20 week long serial that kept children coming back week after week.

Men bought their hardware at either Smith-Murchison or Keeland Hardware; feed and planting supplies were found at one of three such establishments scattered throughout the business community. Gentlemen bought their clothing from Millar and Berry Men's Clothing but often the customers there derived more pleasure from their visits to the store than they did from their purchases. Cartwright's and Thompson' s supplied the ladies in town with their wardrobes, often making the first new fashion statements such as new hemline styles even before local ladies read about them in Harper's Bazaar. The service businesses in town included the Crockett Hotel and Restaurant, The Texas Café, Morrow's Café. and The Royal Restaurant for everything from blue plate special lunches to wonderful Sunday luncheons. We had our shoes repaired at Parker's, our clothing cleaned at Joe Arledge's Tailor Shop and Dry Cleaners. We took care of our appearances at one of four barber shops and five beauty shops, ordered flowers from the two florists and got out of town shipments via the local Railway Express office. Asher's was the only shoe store in town and the place where every child knew an all-day sucker awaited him when his new school shoes were bought. For home furnishing needs, everybody went to Knox Furniture Store, where you could buy all types of furniture and the latest appliances. The east side of the business district was fringed with churches; there was the First Baptist Church with its huge black dome, The First Methodist Church with its bell tower entrance facing two streets and the big white frame First Christian Church, just across the street from the Methodist Church.

We had everything one could possibly want wrapped up in a space of six to seven square blocks. All this was centered by the impressive courthouse which sat in the middle of red brick streets where six state highways converged on our courthouse square. Our town was a showplace indeed. We even had picture postcards of our courthouse square because it was so modern, beautifully designed and well maintained.

Some of the luckiest children in Crockett were the ones whose parents allowed them to buy ice cream cones at The Silver Grill. Now The Silver Grill wasn't a beautiful place to many people, actually it had a rather barren interior except for the oversized calendars from Knox Furniture and Callaway Funeral Home, but to me it was gorgeous. On either side of the room there were benches with small desk-like tops attached to arms dividing the long expanse of wooden benches into methodical eating niches. Centering this grand linoleum-floored establishment was a soda fountain, very old fashioned in a way, but always spotlessly clean. From this hub, my dreams of a banana split materialized, not just any banana split, but one that cried out "Eat Me" from beneath its mountainous topping of gooey syrups and fluffy cream. The Silver Grill was the retreat for high schoolers who congregated there after school. I call them high schoolers because this was before our society labeled anyone between 12 and 20 as teenagers; before the word delinquent was on everybody's lips and before parents needed books and psychiatrists to rear their children properly.

I recall dreaming of how wonderful it was going to be when I was old enough to have a rightful place in the special back room; the sanctuary of my older idols. After I placed my order for an ice cream cone, I felt as monumentally important as the almost grown-ups in the back. When the soda jerk, usually a high school heartthrob, handed me my strawberry cone, I held it securely in my fist, left my vantage point and wandered out the front door filled with fantasies of what I would do when I was allowed to go there every single afternoon after school. As I walked aimlessly toward home, I paused to gaze at the pictures of the upcoming graduates from Crockett High School. The seniors looked very impressive all dressed up in their Sunday best.

I said I walked aimlessly but, I must admit that isn't entirely true for I had pressing matters that simply had to be resolved on my way home. My first stop was the Baptist Church, not for organized activity of any sort but for the privilege of walking up and jumping down the big curving steps at the entrance of the enormous brick house of worship. Sometimes when I was accomplishing this great feat I would ease my head through the massive oak church doors to listen to Mrs. Keissling, the organist, practice hymns and special numbers for Sunday service, but most of the time I would climb the well-worn marble steps and jump back down them one at a time until the soles of my feet tingled with the numbing sensations that told me I'd had enough for one day. With this accomplished, I'd go behind the church, get my bike from the secret spot I'd stashed it and continue my erratic journey home.

Somewhere along the way I was compelled to find a stick, not just a plain old ordinary stick, but the special kind that the wind blew from the big oak trees in Dr. Wootters' yard. This may not sound very important to you but, it was a personal and unbreakable requirement that I find a sturdy stick before I came to the ornate iron fences in front of some of the older homes between downtown and my house. To pass these fences without dragging a stick along them as a terrible omen, almost as bad as stepping on the cracks in the sidewalks, so my search for the appropriate stick had a truly dedicated purpose.

I was likely to stop several more times before reaching my destination depending upon what I saw that demanded my immediate and personal attention. Mrs. Denny might have some new blooms in her flower beds I needed to inspect, or there may be an errant oleander branch growing through the fence which if left unattended would surely block the sidewalk in front of the Adams' home. Naturally, I had to stop long enough to break that tender green nuisance off its otherwise perfectly shaped bush. If I felt the need of more activity, I rode my bike up and down the steep hill several more times than necessary . Given these imperatives, you can see I was a very, very busy little girl.

As I turned the corner of the street where I lived, I pedaled my blue Western Flyer bike as fast as my legs would move so I could kick up the gravel in the driveway when I stepped on the brakes with all my might. In this attention getting manner, I announced my arrival home. Right away Mother asked where I had been and what I had been doing, although she never really waited for an answer because she knew about all the important missions I performed on my homeward trip. After I checked in with Mother, I was duty bound to visit my grandmother, who lived next door. After all, Mama probably had baked some butter cookies with homemade jelly centers and it was my solemn obligation as a grandchild to eat some of them while they were still warm. The fact that I loved both Mama and her cookies had much to do with my dutiful visit. I always went in the back door of Mama and Poppa's house; everyone did. There was a certain warmth about this back door, the top half of it was glass and it opened into a huge kitchen which smelled at various time of homemade jelly, chicken and dressing, fried chicken, lemon loaf cake or a million other things nobody else in the world prepared the way Mama Charm did. Charm, by the way, was her real name, and though I don't know how my great-grandparents thought of it, the name was perfect for this lovable forebear of mine. She was a real charmer in every sense of the word. Three of Mother's five brothers still lived at home at this time, so there was always something cooking in that big friendly kitchen. Since Mama had a cook to prepare dishes not needing her special attention, she always found time to read stories to me and to tell me about things my Mother did when she was a little girl.

One summer I moved my entire wardrobe all the way next door to my grandparents' house and lived with them the entire three months. What a wonderful experience I had living in the same room which had been my Mother's. The most excitement was provided by the full-length mirror on the closet door. Often I would stand in front of the big reflector making all the ugly faces at my command, at other times, I'd wrap my body in a lap throw pretending to be an Indian princess and still later dance around the room imitating Ginger Rogers' latest movie performance.

Summer was always a treasured time of the year because of the exciting things we did only in the warmer weather. The whole family, as well as some of the neighbors, gathered on my grandparents' front porch every Sunday afternoon. While the grown ups talked and visited, the not quite grown ups played baseball ; the smaller children played tag or hide and seek. About mid afternoon, Mama would ask the men for volunteers to crank the ice cream freezer. Everyone knew it would not be too long before we would eat so much of Mama's fresh peach ice cream our throats would be almost frozen from the experience. As the men cranked the freezer, one of the children sat atop it so the wooden freezer wouldn't walk away. Usually two children alternated the sitting duties, but only when the first one screamed it was too cold on his or her bottom side. Emoting about frozen posteriors was almost as much of a thrill as licking the dasher, and everybody knew that was the very best ice cream there was.

As day turned to dusk, the grown ups rocked and talked of recent events, the near grown ups went their separate ways and the children ran about the yard catching lightening bugs, carefully placing them in ventilated jars to light up their bedside tables as the children drifted off to dreamland. It was a perfect ending to a calm summer Sunday.

Dreams Had Come
True But Then....

Our town had accomplished so much in the last few years. Mayor Jack Beasley had spearheaded the drive to improve our community. The Chamber of Commerce, the civic organizations and the City of Crockett had reason to celebrate; after all, they had staged the largest parade ever held in Crockett for the observance of the 1936 Texas Centennial. I got to ride on one of the floats so I didn't get to see the parade, but I do remember everyone in town was excited about the event. As I recall, the procession began near our home on Grace Street, wound through downtown at a snail's pace and was brought to a close in front of the Davy Crockett Memorial Building in City Park.

The park was the jewel of Crockett; Jack Beasley's dream had come true. It covered acres of land, every inch of which was enclosed with low treated-log fences entwined with beautiful red rambling roses. There was a bandstand on the west side of the park. The elegant colonial style Memorial Building was reflected in the pool in front of it and nearby was the stone and bronze marker honoring David Crockett. To the east was an Exhibits Building for County Fairs, and a Livestock Building where prized and prize-winning animals were shown off during the fair and where animal auctions were held at other times. Adjacent to the Exhibits Building was a large picnic area and playground. Each picnic area had a concrete table and seats, as well as a rock grill providing the perfect spot for preparing such picnic delights as hot dogs and hamburgers. At times, there was so much activity in the park it seemed difficult to find space for another family gathering.

The Chamber of Commerce printed a brochure exclaiming the virtues of Crockett praising the agricultural excellence, the educational advantages, the business climate, the recreational facilities and the religious and cultural institutions that all contributed to the community. This was distributed far and wide in an attempt to help our city grow. Pride in our town was evident everywhere you looked. New street signs were erected and the new Houston County Courthouse was planned. The replacement for the courthouse which had burned was going to cost over $200,000, according to my grandfather, and was going to built of white marble. Wow, we were going to have the prettiest town in all of Texas. Our local high school football team was the pride of the whole town and our band members performed better each time they played. School Superintendent Deck had amassed a faculty of teachers who were overseeing the education of the young with dedication and determination. I knew more of the high schoolers than most of my friends did because they were friends of my uncles, Pud and Smith and my cousin Collin Jr. All three of them were in the final years of their local education.

When he was in high school, Pud planned a party to be held at Mama and Poppa's house. Mama busily prepared food for the affair for several days. All of Pud's friends in the Senior class were coming to his dinner party.

Though I don't recall the circumstances, he somehow convinced Mother to let me stay for the party. I felt so grown when Mother agreed to let me part of my uncle's special night.

All the goodies Mama served disappeared quickly and soon the real party began. Pud, Delbert, Bill and some of the other boys rolled back the rugs in the living room and dining room, brought out a hand cranked portable record player and a stack of records and assigned me the job of keeping the music going. They had more important things to do, they were going to spend their time dancing with the pretty girls. And they danced and danced and danced for what seemed a lifetime to me, because after each record ended, I had to turn off the player, rewind it and locate the next song they were all telling me to find.

"Play 'Scatterbrain" Carol"

"I like 'In the Mood' "

"How about putting on 'Elmer's Tune,' that's a real good one."

Gloria Van Pelt, who was Miss Everything at school, tried to help me keep the music going a couple of times but, was always pulled away by another young Romeo waiting his turn to dance with her. The meal and the dancing must have been a huge success because the guests were still enjoying themselves when Mother and Daddy said it was time for me to go home. Although I hated to leave the party and miss any of the fun, I was more than willing to relinquish my job as chief winder-upper of the record player. My arm was sore the next day but I wore my aching muscles like a badge of honor when I told my friends I had been to a party with the high school seniors. It was my pals' consensus that I was pretty important to be allowed to go to such a function. I did nothing to discourage them from asking me to repeat who was hugging and kissing on whom as they danced. I walked with a strut for days after Pud's party, after all I was special, or at least that was how my uncle had made me feel.

Smith and his buddies were involved in the usual pastimes boys seemed to enjoy most. He often went hunting with Herbert, Claude and Jamie hoping to kill enough quail for a feast with all the trimmings. At other times, they built tremendous kites which they would get into the air only by pulling them behind the jalopies they held together with baling wire and hope. My youngest uncle fancied himself a musician. He played trombone in the band and practiced his sliding instrument while sitting on the front porch. Sometimes, Smith was joined by Pud and Collin Jr., both playing the saxophone but, more often than not all I heard was the trombone part of a march the band would perform at the next football game. While he was pretty good at playing the long silver contraption, the part he played was never the melody so I couldn't tell what song it was most of the time. He must have become rather frustrated with the situation of playing only the harmonic parts because before long, he bought an accordion. This squeeze box, as he called it, afforded him the opportunity to play all the parts and I could finally identify the songs he played. Not all the songs were beautiful but, I found those he mastered to be very entertaining, especially when he played "The Three Little Fishes' and "Beautiful, Beautiful Texas" and allowed me to sing along with him.

Going to the picture show was the major form of entertainment in Crockett. Our family went almost as frequently as the movie changed, usually twice a week, and when I didn't go with my parents, I attended the matinees with my grandmother. She loved movies but, had to go during the day because Poppa would not go with her at night. Everyone in town anticipated the arrival of " Gone With the Wind." the most popular film of the day and certainly the longest show I had ever attended. It was so long there was an intermission after the first half of the movie which ended with Scarlett O'Hara proclaiming, "As God is my witness, I will never go hungry again." Mother loved the film, it fit into her dramatic repertoire very nicely. During the intermission , I heard my parents and their friends commenting how they could not believe the risque language they had read would be used at the end of the movie epic. Bad language simply wasn't used in family entertainment; it was not polite. Nevertheless, at the end of the picture Clark Gable uttered Rhett Butler's famous words, "Frankly my dear, I don't give a damn." There were gasps throughout the theater. They had seen it and heard it and they still didn't believe. What was becoming of good taste?

Many of the movies that debuted the same year became classics: "Mr. Smith Goes to Washington" "Wuthering Heights, "The Hound of the Baskervilles," "Gunga Din" and "Goodbye Mr. Chips" to name a few.

As impressive as the movies were, however, the newsreels of events from around the world were almost as important to the moviegoers. Newspapers and certainly LIFE magazine were excellent ways to keep abreast of what was going on in the world outside our little Utopia but, seeing and hearing the newsreels provided us with a different perspective. We saw quick, well-narrated stories of the good works being accomplished across the country in CCC (Civilian Conservation Corps) camps, the parade of bathing beauties competing for the Miss America pageant title, the gala opening of "Gone With the Wind" in Atlanta, and announcements that the economy was improving to help our country recover from the depression.

With greater frequency each month, we saw pictures of soldiers from a country called Germany. There seemed to be an endless number of them in each film clip and they marched in a most peculiar way. They called their marching the" goose step" and they saluted their leader by raising their right hands as stiffly as they marched. This was the way they honored Der Fuhrer, as they referred to Chancellor Adolph Hitler. Pictures of the German children reflected smaller versions of the soldiers, for they wore short-panted uniforms and marched in the same unusual manner. They most assuredly were cadets but a far cry from the ones I read about in "Gasoline Alley" in the funny papers.

President Roosevelt declared that Thanksgiving Day would be celebrated on the fourth Thursday in November, rather than the last Thursday of the month as had been the tradition. Poppa said he thought it was ridiculous to consider changing a national holiday, especially since he felt it was being done on to give merchants more shopping time between Thanksgiving and Christmas. It seemed like a very good idea to me because it meant we would have Mama's turkey and dressing and all the trimmings earlier than we had in the past.

In the months to come our family listened to more news on the radio than we had previously. Mother and Daddy particularly like hearing a reporter named Edward R. Murrow who always began his reports with "This is London," and closed each broadcast with "Good night and good luck." The newsman referred to the Blitzkrieg, which he explained meant lightning war, when Germany sent armored troops into other countries without warning. Neville Chamberlain resigned as Britain's Prime Minister. He was replaced by Winston Churchill who in a dramatic and patriotic speech declared, "I have nothing to offer but blood, toil, tears and sweat." As these events took place I heard my parents and their friends discuss war much more often. Daddy said we would soon be right in the middle of the fighting. There was less talk of happy things and much more conversation regarding war. I found it scary.

Toward the end of the summer, Pud was preparing to go to college in Waco, I was looking forward to my second year of school. Mother had already purchased my school clothes for the upcoming year on one of our frequent train trips to Houston. Collin Jr. was practicing football for the upcoming season. Uncle Ben had returned from college to work at Poppa's wholesale grocery business. Uncle George and Aunt Helen were about to move into their new house two doors down from ours and Bubba would soon celebrate his first birthday. Daddy came home from work talking about reports that Germany had invaded Poland. He seemed to think this was very important and could lead to war for us. I didn't know where Poland was but, I knew about Germany and the funny looking soldiers I had seen in the newsreels. When Daddy finished reading The Houston Chronicle the next night, he asked Mother to be sure to keep the paper in a safe place. This paper would one day be a piece of history he wanted to preserve for his children. At the time I thought Daddy's interest in the paper was pretty silly, after all, he usually kept papers only to light campfires when he and Uncle Collin went fishing. In the next few weeks I heard the grown ups discussing war more and more. Great Britain, France and Russia, wherever that was, had all declared war on Germany. What was coming next?

Headlines of the newspapers screamed with big banners when troops from both Britain and France were evacuated from Dunkirk. LIFE and the newsreels depicted the massive efforts to rescue the fighting men who had been hopelessly trapped by Hitler's troops. Every kind of boat one could imagine had been pressed into service

19

in heroic attempts to get the Allies back to England. Again Churchill address the world via radio saying, "We shall not flag or fail. We shall fight in France, we shall fight on the seas and oceans, we shall fight with growing confidence and growing strength in the air, we shall defend our island, whatever the cost may be, we shall fight on the beaches, we shall fight on the landing grounds, we shall fight in the fields and in the street, we shall fight in the hills; we shall never surrender." The Allies needed a battle cry after Dunkirk because 30,000 men were either killed or captured during that one encounter. Churchill had provided just that.

The talk of war increased everywhere I overheard adults talking. Poppa said it was Europe's problem, we would not get involved. After all, he added, according to the Bible, there would always be wars and rumors of war. The World War that ended in 1918 would be the last World War, according to my grandfather. This was one war we had better stay out of; it simply wasn't any of our business.

Paris fell to the Germans, Italy declared war on Great Britain and France. It was getting worse. By this time, all the kids had learned how gallant the Royal Air Force was because we had seen the newsreels and were learning more about what war was about. In retaliation to Hitler's Luffwaffe air attacks on London, the RAF began night bombing raids on German targets. The Battle of Britain reached its peak when German planes attacked by dropping hundreds of bombs on England. To make matters even worse, the Germans equipped their bombs with devices which whistled as they were falling towards their targets. That meant everyone could hear what was headed their way.

We saw pictures of English children being guided into bomb shelters by their parents. I tried to relate to the fear and uncertainty I saw in their young eyes. Why would anybody on Earth be cruel enough to want to hurt children? I dreamed about these children and how frightened they must be; I was glad I wasn't there.

The RAF had saved Britain. At this time, Mr. Churchill praised the English flier by saying, "Never in the field of human conflict was so much owed by so many to so few." When Mother and Daddy read that in the newspapers they agreed his speech would go down in history as one of the greatest ever. Apparently the Prime Minister's speeches infuriated the Axis , as Germany and Italy were known by this time, because the Luftwaffe began what came to known as the Blitz—all night German air raids on London. What was to happen to those children?

In the meantime, Franklin Roosevelt announced he would run for an unprecedented third term as President of the United States. My family discussed this issue at great length. It was unheard of for a man to hold our highest office that long; on the other hand, it didn't make sense to change horses in mid stream when it seemed so very likely we might get into the war ourselves. Americans voted their convictions in November when FDR was reelected by a huge majority.

What was Hitler waiting for? When was he going to cross the English Channel? Surely if the German dictator had rolled through most of Europe in a few short months, he will not be stopped by a mere 30 miles of water. Millions of Americans asked these questions but, at the same time remained fearful of what the answer might be.

As a diversion from all the talk of war, we went to the movies, where we were entertained by "The Grapes of Wrath." "The Philadelphia Story," "The Mark of Zorro" and two films made especially for children. Walt Disney brought more story book magic to life , the way he had done with "Snow White and the Seven Dwarfs," when he released "Pinocchio" and "Fantasia." Soon after the movies came out all the kids were singing their songs, especially "When You Wish Upon a Star." One of our favorite sayings became "Jimminey Cricket!" We used the expression which was the name of a character from Pinocchio every way we could.

"Jimminey Cricket, that was great."

"Jimminey Cricket, you shouldn't do that."

"Jimminey Cricket, your mom's going to be mad about that tear in your pants!"

Perhaps we thought this an acceptable way to swear and get by with it, because our parents didn't seem to mind us using the term. We loved it. It seemed to be a year for kids because three of the most popular songs were being sung by every kid I knew. The easy to learn lyrics of "San Antonio Rose," and "You Are My Sunshine"were sung at birthday parties and at Scout meetings around the campfire but, my choice was a song recorded by a revered cowboy star, Gene Autry. "Back in the Saddle Again" was on every child's hit parade, not just mine.

Daddy often talked about buying a new car, he even showed me pictures of a new Chevrolet he said he'd like to have but, it cost $695 so he'd have to wait awhile before he could get one. He told Mother that owning a Packard was completely out of question; it would cost over $1,000. Not long after he had shown me his dream car, Daddy showed me a picture of the strangest looking car I had ever seen; it was call a general purpose vehicle and had what was called four-wheel drive, whatever that was. In a short period of time, this odd looking car, if you could call it that, would be known all over the world as a Jeep.

As the war wore on in Europe, Daddy's collection of important newspapers grew, GERMANY INVADES RUSSIA was the headline of one of them. Regardless of what else was going on in the world, adults always seemed to return to talk about the war. President Roosevelt called for, and Congress approved, a Lend Lease program so we could send badly needed medical supplies, food and war supplies to Britain, in return for leasing land from them for U.S. bases in the future. Now my family really got worried that we were going to get in the war no matter what. It was a question now of when it was going to happen.

Young men were paying close attention to articles in the paper which advised them that within 30 days after the United States declared war, if it ever does, young Johnny Jones, able-bodied, unmarried and about 25 will be in the army. They would be the first men drafted for military service. Thank goodness Pud and Smith weren't 25 yet, or they might be going to war. Such articles continued to be published. They urged high school graduates to go into the Army Air Corps as aviation cadets. Other news items encouraged them to sign up with the Navy recruiter, whose office was located in the Post Office Building. High school graduates? I wondered, would my uncles go to war after all?

Thanksgiving came and went, there was still more talk of war. I was beginning to believe war was the only subject grown ups knew to talk about anymore. I don't think they realized how much time they were devoting to the dreadful business of war talk. It was troubling me to see those I loved so concerned.

Mama Charm was preparing for Christmas but, then she had been busy with her plans since the first of October. While Mama derived much pleasure from time spent with each individual member of the family, nothing provided her greater satisfaction than having the whole brood together, especially at Christmas. During the holiday season, she became a pure pixie who filled our young hearts with dreams of toys and Santa Claus' visit. Christmas was not a mere holiday to Mama, it was a three month season. In early October, she began slicing candied fruit and cutting nuts into small pieces ultimately turning out fruit cakes of every variety. Since Poppa was a teetotaler, liquor was never allowed in his home. This posed a significant problem for Mama, her cakes just wouldn't be aged properly unless a tablespoon of whiskey was drizzled over their surfaces at least once a week prior to Christmas. To solve this problem, Daddy had to smuggle a small bottle of contraband booze into the house for her every Fall. By the time Christmas rolled around, the china cabinet in the dining room smelled like a distillery but, the cakes were always moist and delicious. I now realize the whiskey cakes couldn't possibly have been a secret; Poppa simply wouldn't spoil Mama's childlike deception.

Long before Thanksgiving Mama had stashed away gifts for every member of the family. She personally oversaw the creation of the one perfect front door wreath. By the first of December Christmas cards were written to friends near and far, and I do mean written, for each one carried a different and very personal note of good wishes and holiday cheer. Her kitchen was filled with aromas peculiar to the season as she lovingly prepared every delicious goody we would share at Christmas; fudge, stuffed dates, orange nut bread, cranberry sauce and finally on Christmas morning turkey and dressing. She worked at an almost frantic pace preparing for the holidays, never failing to enjoy every moment of her loving efforts.

Thanksgiving dinner was usually highlighted with wild turkey as our main course. Poppa managed to shoot at least one turkey each year so the family could enjoy

Thanksgiving dinner not too unlike the very first one. He and his hunting buddies Jim McLean, Dr. Paul Stokes, C. H. Callaway, Lanier Edmiston, Raymond Cornelius and Loch Cook often returned from their hill country hunting lease near Kerrville with lots of turkeys and a record number of deer. One year they bagged so many deer, they hung them in front of Mr. Parker's store and proudly posed for a picture with their kill.

Some of the most memorable times of my early years are the trips I took with my grandparents. The first one I remember was to Central Texas where Poppa was searching for a new deer lease for his hunting companions. No matter where we ate, I always ordered exactly what Poppa ordered. On one particular trip Poppa resolved one of the more perplexing problems of my young life. Smith and I were occupying the back seat of Poppa's black Chevy; a situation not pleasing to my young uncle and positively miserable for me. After hours of being unable to see out the window, I tired of staring at the twisted rope coat rack dangling from the back of the driver's seat and became very verbal regarding my displeasure. After I had driven Smith to the point of wanting to scream, Poppa pulled the car off the road, got a suitcase from the trunk, placed it on the back seat, topped it with a pillow and sat me atop the whole contraption. As quickly as that, my dilemma was over; my trip changed from a real bore to a wonderful adventure.

Whenever we saw something of interest, an historical marker, or a pretty roadside park, we paused to enjoy the man made as well as the natural beauties along the way.

Somehow, people today don't have or don't take time to enjoy these roadside pleasantries. My grandparents made certain I learned to appreciate such marvelous things as a shady picnic spot, cold water from a natural spring, fields of delicate bluebonnets bowing in a soft spring breeze and the gracefulness of deer jumping across the road we were traveling. We ended the first day of our trip to Fredericksburg where we stayed at the Nimitz. Hotel. The owner's son was an Admiral in the U. S. Navy, so there were pictures of ships and men in uniform all over the lobby. We were impressed with all the military mementos. After Poppa made arrangements for his hunting companions the next day, we continued our trip, moving on to activities I found more enjoyable. One stop was a cave where I saw gigantic stone columns that Poppa told me were created by tiny drops of water dripping in the same place for hundreds maybe even thousands of years. I didn't know how much older they were than Poppa but he assured me they were much, much older than he was.

We rode on to Washington on the Brazos where Mama explained the Republic of Texas was founded. She said at one time Texas was a whole different country instead of just one of the United States. My grandparents knew all this kind of stuff and often told me they had studied any number of subjects even after they had several children. They were the only people I knew who had studied school subjects after they were grown. Poppa shared lots of history and geography with me, but almost always ended his conversation about each topic with a lecture on the importance of a good education. He wanted me

27

to learn everything I could because he hadn't had the opportunity of more than a third grade experience with formal schooling.

He and his friends went hunting that year. As usual he was successful and took great pride in providing a wild turkey for the family's Thanksgiving dinner once more.

CORNER DRUGSTORES

No small town in the 40's was complete without a drug store owned and managed by a pharmacist who was both chemist and confidant. My home town had five drug stores, but our family usually shopped at one of two run by a duo of the warmest humans who ever lived in Crockett. Mr. Carl and Big Dan, as everyone in town called them, were friendly competitors who served their community with the devotion of those who had taken the Hippocratic oath.

Mr. Carl's store was on the courthouse square around which came the through traffic of the six highways leading into town. The owner was a man capable of doing an unlimited number of things well, but to the children his most important job was serving as a sort of doctor of minor ills. I suppose most of us had our sore throats swabbed in the back of his store at one time or another. In barefoot season, he was often busy bandaging sore toes or minor cuts and scratches, painful reminders of ungraceful falls from bicycle and skating accidents. At other times, he cared for our boils, sties and splinters; each with the care of a physician and attentiveness of a loving parent. It wasn't as though Mr. Carl had set himself up in a sort of medical practice, no that wasn't it at all; it was just that nobody's mother could care for a minor hurt the way he did. He was reassuring when he bandaged my ankle after I had mangled it in my bike chain. Although it really wasn't a serious injury, I was the envy of every neighborhood child who saw the professionally administered dressing on my arrival home. I don't know about his other patients, but I always felt very important when sporting one of his bandages. Status among my peers was the main reason I asked Mother to let Mr. Carl care for my little hurts. In Goolsby's Drug Store every splinter in a tiny finger, every scrapped knee and every cut lip was treated with affection as well as medication, no matter how many prescriptions my hero had to fill or how far behind he was in finishing his pharmaceutical inventory.

There was a consistent warmhearted and neighborly sense of sociability about this store, especially at the soda fountain. Other merchants had their morning coffee and afternoon cold drinks at the fountain and almost everyone sipped a Coke while shopping or waiting for a prescription to be filled. It was the delight of regular customers to confuse a new soda jerk by ordering concoctions with which he was not familiar.

The joke often turned out to be on the snickering customers when they were served terrible combinations of syrup and soda defying human consumption. One constant at the soda fountain was the chicken salad sandwiches; Mrs. Goolsby's recipe was made fresh each day and everyone in town knew "Miss Helen'" was the best, bar none.

While the two druggists were similar in their devotion to the welfare of their customers, each had a different personality distinctively his own.

Big Dan was a short, rotund man with a round and gentle face, usually exuding the warmest, most contagious smile in town. Sometimes, his twinkling eyes would reflect the impish good nature that was his most lovable quality; at other times, those same eyes were the mirrors of the joys and sorrows of his friends or the visual sounding board for some child's latest reason for needing a handful of those intriguing empty capsules he kept in the huge bottles on the prescription counter. Other businessmen in town enjoyed pulling elaborate pranks on Big Dan then stand back and listen as the kindhearted pharmacist stuttered his red faced retort. Half the fun of teasing Mr. Julian was getting his answer, for whenever he became excited, pressured or embarrassed, the man stuttered something fierce.

Julian's soda fountain had no stools, just a foot rail. For the ladies who didn't wish to sidle up to the fountain, there were three or four old-fashioned marble topped ice cream table with those delightful bent wood chairs that groaned a bit every time someone sat in them. Centering each of these tables was a cone shaped container of candy striped straws, usually emptied shortly after school children came by for afternoon snacks. The soda goodies weren't limited to these spots though, for during late spring, summer and early fall Big Dan's customers also enjoyed curb service to the few parking spaces in front of his establishment. Mama, Mother and I stopped by frequently for a frosted Coke to be served by Joe Warren and later Jasper Jones. As we sat in the car enjoying our tasty refreshments, Big Dan and his wife, Lois, would step out to visit for awhile, or someone who was shopping might stop to discuss how much they had enjoyed a recent tea, school program , or church affair. I suppose this sounds like pretty boring stuff these days when we are so concerned with missile races, delinquency, drug abuse and world events, but there was a kind of amiability about these sidewalk chats that just isn't around anymore, even when friends are making every effort to be casual and sincere.

Big Dan's type store is nonexistent now. It was a long skinny store with massive fixtures on either side and several glass display cases in the center. The top half of the wooden fixtures against the walls were huge sliding glass doors framed with mahogany stained oak. The doors roared with the sound of springtime thunder whenever Lois showed a customer the newest Evening in Paris set or the latest Coty cologne. Beneath these glass expanses were drawers, hundreds of drawers of all sizes. Each one had a card above it its musty brass pull that supposedly indexed the contents of that particular drawer. I say supposedly because the drawer marked corn pads invariably held aspirin, while the aspirin drawer usually held nail scissors or baby pacifiers; but for all this cross filing, Big Dan could locate exactly what was needed right away. It was very different in his pharmacy, there each bottle or carton was labeled with the preciseness of a seasoned accountant.

There were heaven only knows how many assorted cigar boxes filled with old prescriptions, as dusty as they were yellowed, but still vitally important when some customer asked for a refill of a dosage Dr. Stokes or Dr. Wootters has prescribed for an earache three years ago. We had no pediatricians or other medical specialists in Crockett, just plain old country doctors who knew all their patients well enough to know they wouldn't call every time they had a tummy ache. Folks who were ailing just got a refill of the last medicine the doctor had given them for a like ailment; it that didn't work, then and only then, they went to the doctor's office. Actually the doctors didn't seem to object when patients did this because they were so busy with delivering babies, emergencies and operations, they appreciated anyone who could get the relief needed from a medication refill. Lightening the professional load of the local doctors was one of the main reasons Big Dan had those endless numbers of old, discolored recipes for medicines.

The high point of my visit to Julian's was watching Big Dan prepare one of these medicinal wonders. I was overwhelmed as I watched his chubby hands carefully measured powders on his scales, blend powdery mixtures on a small piece of white marble, divide the prescription into equal parts, then cautiously place each portion in a piece of powder paper. Sometimes, he put his talcum -like cures in capsules, explaining to me that he only used these when the dosage really tasted terrible. The scales he used were not the streamlined type which came later, but rather like a glass shoe box with a collection of precisely marked weights resting below the balance arm of the apparatus. Even though these devices are obsolete tody, I'm sure no more accurate measurements are made now than were made by Big Dan on his aged gauge.

Even my drugstores changed once the war was declared. Past soda jerks were now serving as submariners, paratroopers, airmen, sailors and radiomen. Dr. Carl B.

Goolsby Jr. was now in the Army Medical Corps and Little Dan Julian, now a naval officer. Conversations at the soda fountain turned to war news of the day and were often shared with former fountain employees who were now home of leave. A growing expression of anxiety shadowed the smiles of both Big Dan and Mrs. Carl as the war continued and their offspring were so very far from home. One of the best selling items in both stores during the war years were service flags. These small banners were displayed proudly in the windows of those with loved ones in the service of their country. The flags had one blue star for each serviceman from the home. Sadly, there were different ones that began to appear as the war progressed; they were the gold star flags indicating that someone in the family had paid the ultimate price for our freedom.

These are memories of the corner drug stores in my town. Neither was on a corner, neither was beautifully decorated, neither was a supermarket type establishment with garden equipment, paint and housewares; but, both were filled to the walls with all the love, understanding and good humor my two heroes possessed. As I look back, I realize that my affinity for these stores was determined by the radiant personalities of their owners. Without these men, my town as it was then would not be so vividly ensconced in my memories.

Swings, Clubs And Other Good Stuff

I'm sure few youngsters these days know what a sandbag swing is, yet this was one of the most popular playthings when I was a child. Parents understood how vitally important it was to have a sack swing hanging from the first substantial limb on the largest tree in the yard. It was imperative that Mother buy a tremendous sack of flour, for nothing in the world made a swing as good as a flour sack. There was the extreme pleasure I derived from pestering Mother to use all the flour as quickly as possible; step one in my anticipation of pleasures to come.

After Mother finally used the flour, and it seemed to take simply eons for that flour to disappear, I finally got the priceless, tightly woven sack for my very own. Step two in the master plan was to painstakingly fill the treasured receptacle with sand from Mother's flower beds where the grounds wasn't so hard, tie a knot in the top of it and annoy Daddy 'til he surrendered, bought some rope and put up the swing. The day Daddy put up my first sack swing was almost as important to me as signing the Declaration of Independence. Believe me, I was John Hancock.

The neighborhood children watched with wonder as Daddy tested my remarkable plaything, each impatiently waiting a turn on it once Daddy finally declared it to be safe. These swings were useful for many other purposes besides swinging; they were perfect weapons of defense when somebody chased you; for the boys, they also doubled as punching bags. Most of the time, however, I just used mine as a swing; the most wonderful one in the world. At times my dangling friend was a jungle vine for every screaming young Tarzan on the block, or the latest airplane for all the would-be pilots nearby. When I tired of swinging or throwing it at someone, my simple toy was also the weight necessary to anchor the rope as I climbed up, touched the limb it was tied to and slid back down the rope. Now I ask you, what kind of fun can a child have with a modern swing bolted together on a steel stand. Who ever heard of sliding down a chain?

When I wasn't on my swing, I found plenty of diversions to occupy my time. Our back yard was surrounded by a big hedge, not a special kind of hybrid hedge with an unpronounceable name, just a plain old ordinary privet hedge. This oversized greenery was the one nearby object with endless possibilities; it was really something special, except of course when Mother pulled a switch from it and either threatened to use it or did when I failed to mind. When is was used for disciplinary purposes, I wished my beloved shrubbery had not been so handy. Most of the time, however, my hedge was an extremely important source of amusement. My next door playmate, Vira Jo, and I made bracelets and crowns from twisted hedge branches, and nothing, but nothing drew hopscotch outlines in the dirt better than a large hedge limb. At other times its leaves decorated the orange crate table we used for backyard tea parties featuring our very special brand of mud pies lightly frosted with flower bed sand.

The year Daddy failed to trim the bushes, which were already taller than our one-story house, the hedges became gigantic. Vira Jo and I worked for days cutting a section from the very midst of the monster hedge and built a playhouse in the center of our verdant tangle. Ours was a beautiful abode handsomely furnished with tables and chairs made of orange crates and apple boxes. Unfortunately, because these furnishings weren't padded, by the end of the day Mother usually had to de-splinter my legs and what she described as the back of my lap. Occasionally one of those terribly obtrusive slivers managed to work its way through my clothes and into my tender bottom. Even though Mother removed it, the almost invisible particle caused me more than a little discomfort when I sat down for supper.

Today's children know nothing about Shirley Temple curls and Spanky skull caps. In the late thirties and early forties, nearly every young girl's mother wanted her child to look like Shirley Temple, who was the darling of the whole world at the time. No matter how long her hair or how unlike Little Miss Lollipop a child's features might be, young girls eventually wound up with copy cat versions of those world famous tresses. These hairdos caused some of the weirdest sights even seen in my town, or for that matter in outer space. Each mother had a unique method of rolling her moppet's hair, but no matter what system was used the little girl was a truly peculiar looking creature when her hair was set. Some rolled curls on wire rollers, some on brown kidskin curlers, some on socks, some with hair pins and some with a variety of other items of disfigurement.

Each Saturday every girl in town had her hair rolled so she'd look beautiful for Sunday School. Of course, this meant that swinging, skating or doing anything else that was really fun was forbidden, taboo and out of the question on Saturday afternoon. For this reason my Saturday afternoons were often spent playing Monopoly, dressing and undressing my "Gone With the Wind" paper dolls, drawing pictures of Donald Duck, practicing my piano scales or, on occasion, pouting in my room when Mother absolutely ignored my pitiful pleas to go outside for a bike ride. One unblemished summer afternoon, Mother went shopping leaving me with my grandmother. As soon as Mother was out of sight, I sneaked out to play with Vira Jo and her visiting cousin; a rebellious act I lived to regret for some time to come. My friends had not had their hair shampooed, so they were playing with the garden hose, dousing each other from head to toe. When I could stand it no longer, I tantalized them with a battery of dares until they finally turned the water on me, saturating my almost dry hair. The outcome of this defiance would not have been so bad it I hadn't stayed out in the sun long enough for dry my locks, but that caused a calamity. Because Mother had rolled my hair on brown kidskin curlers, when she took my hair down I had zebra striped hair. Those wretched curlers colored my otherwise golden tresses with reddish brown stripes all over my head. Mother screamed at me, then tried her best to wash it out, but her efforts were to no avail. The markings had to grow off as surely as they had been dyed into my long blonde hair on purpose. I don't recall who cried more tears over my frightful condition, but between the two of us we must have wept a small Mississippi right there in my room.

Just as curls were all the rage for girls, Spanky skull caps were the fad for boys. Actually there were two widely contrasting trends for boys; their mothers wanted them to be like Freddy Bartholemew with his Little Lord Fauntleroy frilly collar and impeccable manners; their dads and the boys usually convinced mom that an Our Gang skull cap and neighborhood clubhouse fit the offspring's personality much better. Thanks to the great cycloptic medium of television today's kids can share my early interest in Our Gang comedies. Children who grew up before TV had to see these films at the movies, or picture show as it was known then. After seeing these films, the boys bought skull caps, parting with them only long enough to bathe and go to church.

After each new Our Gang comedy, we began plans to build or redecorate our clubhouse. Some of these very exclusive private clubs were in trees, others in storage rooms. Most of them, however, were constructed of scrap lumber tacked on the back of garages with childish hope and blunt nails being used for the third or fourth time. One such clubhouse was the private property of L.A., a skull cap clad pal of mine. What a wonder it was. The entrance was covered with a drapery of feed sacks. Over the door was sign which read KEEP OUT. MEMBURS ONLY. Near the door was the ever present skull and crossbones flag flying from a broken fishing pole, the souvenir from a fishing excursion with my friend's Dad. When I became a member of this discriminating club, I was given a solemn oath of allegiance to the other members, promising never in my whole life to reveal our top secret password. It was only after this elaborate ceremony that I was finally allowed to enter the clubhouse. Inside were two buckets turned upside down, the ultra modern seating on either side of a magnificent table made of two apple boxes topped with three pieces of odd length 1x10's.

One wall featured a list of club members and their duties as officers; everyone was an officer. A year old calendar hung on the adjoining wall above an orange crate filled with cigar boxes, one for the valuables of each club member.Somewhere in the secret edifice was a hidden niche the treasurer used to store our weekly two cent dues in a fruit jar until we needed to spend our funds for having a picnic. If you think our club had no purpose, you are wrong. We had a very important mission, for at each weekly meeting members exchanged comic books. Sometimes, if you were very lucky, two Little Lulu books would get you Captain Marvel or a Batman; on other occasions, one Superman would net a trade of three Mickey Mouses and one Donald Duck. Your trading clout hinged on whether or not your friends had already read the books while visiting you. We each found it necessary to have an old wallet to hold our important club papers. For this reason, as soon as we talked out mothers into buying dad a new one for Father's Day, we all had billfolds of our very own. The main reason we required these well worn hip pocket shaped leather objects was to have a secure place to keep all our movie stubs, newsprint story books that came with boxes of starch and coupons from Blue Horse school supplies. These were valuable documents demanding a guarded place for safekeeping.

Now that I have mentioned school supply coupons, I feel duty bound to explain to you the complicated process a child endured to acquire enough coupons to win a prize. There was a coupon on each package of paper, tablet, notebook and spelling tablet which various companies made. On the back wrappers of the paper were pictures of the far-beyond-your-fondest-dream prizes which could be yours with the proper amount of tokens. There was never an indication of the number a student should save because the prizes were awarded to those who sent in the largest number. On various occasions doll clothes, marbles, tops, bicycle tire tubes with holes in them and even baby kittens were traded for these juvenile status symbols. Each child was dead certain he or she would win the bicycle or radio illustrated on the notebook paper wrapper. I clipped those precious commodities for four years and all I received for all these months of bartering was a fountain pen with a Blue Horse logo on it. To my chagrin, when I got my treasure, it wouldn't hold ink; nevertheless, saving the coupons had been loads of fun. I must admit there is still a trace of this childlike hope in me for I save all kinds of manufacturers' coupons and promptly return sweepstake entries with dreams of the usually exaggerated grand prize.

Coupons weren't the only things kids saved for prizes. My cousin Collin once saved enough Orange Crush bottle caps to win a bicycle. I am not sure how many thousands of bottle caps he saved, but I can assure you he seemed to have a mountain of them before finally sending them in. Saving these was even more complicated than amassing a treasury of school supply coupons. Before bottle caps could be submitted, one had to remove the cork and flatten each one in such a manner the company could still determine they were genuine. Looking back to this important task, I now see how terribly put upon I was when Collin graciously allowed me the privilege of hammering hundreds of them flat for him. He did promise me a ride on his future bike if I would help. I lived for the day his bike would come, but once around the block was enough for me; my short legs and his boys' bike were not compatible at all.

It is the nature of children to collect things at one time or another. Today the trend seems to be baseball and football cards and Barbie dolls, but considering the fact these must bought with allowance money, I doubt very seriously if any of my contemporaries would have taken up such an expensive hobby. Most of our allowance money was spent on Saturday movies, amusements well worth every precious cent we spent on them. The Texas Theater opened at ll o'clock on Saturday mornings. My friends and I were normally standing in line when the box office opened. We stayed at the show for hours, seeing the same horse opera and weekly serial so many times we had memorized the dialogue by the time we finally staggered blindly from the movie to claim our chariots from the bike rack in front. It was a real disappointment when we had to go out of town or get sick on Saturday. Failure to be there caused us to miss an installment of the serial which usually ran for twenty weeks.

There is no telling how many episodes of space men, super heroes and cowboys we watched end with an explosion, and impending crash or other dilemma. Each one caused us to worry about our adventurous idol for an entire week. Sure enough, the next installment left us with yet another suspenseful reason to be concerned Many times after having seen our all day movie, we would congregate to Dorothy's house and act out, almost word for word, what we had seen at the picture show that day. I will never be convinced movies and TV don't impress children, for I still remember some of the corny lines from the flicks I saw lo those many years ago.

KING COTTON

Unquestionably the economy of my home town was firmly based on the production of cotton. The crop each year provided the livelihoods for those who grew, processed, stored and marketed it. There were five cotton gins in Crockett , as well as one in the western sector of the county. The largest single building in town was a cottonseed oil mill which occupied our longest railroad siding except for the one serving the loading dock of the cotton storage warehouse a block away. Cotton buyers, established in offices all over town, were constantly on the telephone to brokers in Houston.

Thousands of acres of farmland nearby were devoted exclusively to the production of the valuable crop. The excitement of the cotton crop coming in each year was outweighed only by the periodically held county wide political elections. As the cotton was picked, all of it by hand at that time, each cotton picker's bags was emptied into wagons in preparation for the trip to the gin. It was not uncommon in this era for the school year to start much later than it does now, for even the children on farms were expected to do their share of the work necessary to bring in the cotton crop. Since our family lived in town, my indication of the excitement was to spot the first wagon load of cotton slowly edge its way past my grandparents' home. Teams of horses strained each muscle to pull the heavy loads along the shoulders of the highways leading to the gins. Invariably, the wagons were driven by the head hand from the farm. This term did not imply the owner, not even the foreman; no, this was the term designated to owner's most trusted farm hand. He was entrusted with delivery of the precious commodity not only to drive the wagon, but also to insure the owner's cotton was ginned properly once it reached its destination. It became his responsibility to sit on the wagon for hours on end, waiting his turn to unload; a job he would repeat many times before all the cotton was harvested.

As the season opened, there was always a big fuss over which farmer would bring in the first bale of the year. This event was of such importance, the winning bale was assigned a place of honor in front of whichever bank had financed the victorious planter. All the roads from the countryside to town grew white, first with a slight coat of lint; later with so much cotton there appeared to have been a middling snowstorm. This condition didn't last long, however, because soon wagons full of less fortunate, and in some cases downright needy, people would follow the paths taken earlier by the cotton wagons, picking up the cotton that had fallen or blown from the gin bound vehicles. When the scavengers' wagons were fully loaded, they too journeyed to the gin to wait a turn in line for the ginning of their "crop."

As the hundreds of loads were brought to town, the gins went into action. Cotton gins are very noisy establishments and with five of them operating in the same town, they generated noises that could be heard all night long throughout the season. When they were in operation, there was a constant, distant hum in the air that lulled me to sleep each night. The air had a distinctive aroma, for as the cotton was processed, the smell of cottonseed oil permeated the whole town; it was a strange odor somewhat akin to the smell of parched peanuts, but sweeter The mill puffed endlessly to produce cottonseed oil and four times each day sounded its whistle denoting the start and end of the workday as well as the beginning and end of the lunch hour. Nobody needed a clock to determine the time; at seven, twelve, one and five o'clock the mill's whistle echoed across our otherwise quiet and peaceful town.

Soon the cotton warehouse began to fill with bales and bales of cotton awaiting shipment. If the price of cotton dropped, they remained intact; if it went up, large numbers of railroad cars were loaded quickly for new destinations. This final step was the single most important of the entire cotton business, for no matter what the quality or the quantity of cotton a farmer had produced, if he didn't sell it a the right time, he was faced with financial ruin. Fortunes were made and fortunes were lost, but cotton remained king.

The Murray Farm west of town on Highway 21 covered almost 10,500 acres and was known as the "Largest Cotton Plantation in the World." It was so large it had several headquarters where workers lived and machinery was based. On the main highway the Murray empire had offices, a gin, a commissary, numerous houses and various buildings that contained repair shops and power equipment. This farm was the model envied by other cotton farmers because they were always using the latest techniques. At one time, they built a levee to protect their lands from floods and although I don't know how long it was my grandfather said it was over 10 miles long. Folks from miles around drove to see the amazing barrier that had been built to tame the Trinity River's flood waters. The cotton growers were so big even manufacturers of farming equipment used their acreage for testing such items as automated cotton picking machinery.

One of the cotton farmers in our area was a man named Bud Rice. To say Bud was a premiere farmer in the county would have been no understatement. He planted hundreds of acres of cotton every year while creating his own kingdom a few miles east of town. Bud was not the greedy person one has read of in books about the Southern cotton barons, but he did build a world uniquely his own. Visits to his farm stand out in my memory as the only times I ever got a personal glimpse of what it must have been like to live on a cotton plantation of old.

To get to Bud's house, Daddy turned off the highway onto a dirt road deeply rutted by the wheels of the heavy cotton wagons. In route, we passed the schoolhouse/church house Bud built for the families who lived on his land. Along the fences were blackberry vines, often laden with shiny fruit begging to be baked in a cobbler. The approach to the Rice home was a long straight lane framed by enormous old oak trees. Beyond this shady path was a spotlessly clean complex of buildings surrounded by a weedless gravel landscape. While this may not depict the traditional image of a cotton plantation, that's what this agricultural spread was. The house itself was not a grand and glamorous edifice by any means.The simple frame house had a front porch filled with rawhide seated rocking chairs. Its roof extended over the portecochere welcoming guests, as did Bud and his wife Cordie. I never remember a time when one or both of them were not on the porch to greet us. Bud was a colorful character, usually dressed in khaki pants and matching shirt and always sporting a broad brimmed hat resting squarely on his head. His trousers seemed to defy Newton's Law for even though they hung well below his big potbelly, they somehow managed to stay in place. He delighted in telling outlandish tales to the amusement of everyone around, usually laughing harder than anyone else at his own stories. My obese friend got more pleasure from entertaining than anyone else I knew; frequently giving grand parties for his friends, their families and their friends and their families until the farm grounds were covered with people of all ages and interests.

When Bud and Cordie gave a party, it was a fun affair. Grand tables were set up under the gigantic oaks, servants piled them with food it had taken days to prepare. Colorful Japanese lanterns were strung from one building to the next until the grounds took on the appearance of a wonderland. Besides the main house, there were numerous other buildings; the well, the smoke house, the generator shed, the tool shed, the barn and two buildings which were uniquely Bud's. Just south of the farmhouse's back door was a log house with a swept dirt floor. It was the only building on the farm not painted a yellowish orange color trimmed with dark brown. The log building was Bud's men's house, as he called, where he and his buddies played poker and drank moonshine all night long or prepared for bird hunting early the following day.

Since women were not allowed in this cabin I never really knew what it looked like inside, but I imagined it filled with hunting trophies, guns, and other accouterments of manly endeavors. The other "Bud" building was the garage. Nobody else I've ever known had a five car garage topped with a dormitory outfitted to sleep ten or twelve people. That in itself was not what attracted my childhood attention as much as the five shiny Model T Fords, one in each garage section. Since Cordie didn't drive and Bud was always chauffeured by Dan, his main hand, it seemed odd they needed all these cars.

On closer inspection, I found three of the cars were supported by big wooden blocks so their wheels wouldn't touch to ground. I was told when Bud learned Ford was going to stop producing Model T's, he bought five of them. To Bud the Model T was the finest car ever built; even Henry Ford himself was not going to deny Bud the pleasure of having a sparkling new and cherished Model T.

Lucille, the Rice's unmarried daughter, was my Mother's best friend; because of this friendship, I became their surrogate grandchild. At times I'd get to spend several days visiting my make believe grandparents; I was treated not unlike a princess from story books. In the morning I'd awaken to the eerie sounds of guinea hens announcing the break of day. The sound of sausage sizzling in the cast iron skillet and the fragrance of homemade biscuits just out of the oven urged my quick departure from bed.

If the weather was nice I'd get to ride in the wagon with Dan as he took big wooden barrels of water to the field hands. If there was time, we would stop and pick fresh blackberries to be enjoyed with fresh cream later in the day. When it came time to ring the dinner bell, Bud would allow me to ring the signal for the field hands to stop working for a midday meal.

Afternoons were spent helping Cordie bake cookies, fishing in a small pond behind the barn, riding a pony or pretending to drive on of the Rice's beloved Model T's. Imaginary driving was a safe way for a child to occupy her time; there was no way she could start the car. For those of you who may never have seen a Model T, I must explain their dissimilarities to the automobiles of today. In order to start one, somebody had to crank the car. This entailed having a man insert the crank in its rightful place below the radiator and twist with all his might until the vehicle started. Once this was accomplished, he hurriedly got into the open sided car, pushed in the clutch and brake, shifted the gear and was on his way. That is unless he let the clutch out too fast; then the whole process had to be repeated. It is easier today to simply turn the key, but then it is also much less an adventure. Spare tires were attached to the rear of the car with a black rubber shower-cap-like cover bearing the name of the dealer who sold the car. The windshield could be cranked open to let more fresh air flow around the riders on very warm days. Surely the most remarkable feature of all was the car's horn, a far cry from the wimpy beep-beeps we hear on modern cars. The Model T horn was a masterpiece of sound, as totally American as George Gershwin music. The sound of that horn became a symbol of American know-how all over the world as it AOOOOOga-AOOOOOgaed for whatever purpose.

By the time afternoon rolled around, it was time for my bath. Ordinarily this was not a big deal, but taking a bath at the Rice's was special. The servants filled a big claw-footed tub with water heated on a wood-burning stove to just the right temperature. Cordie bathed me and shampooed my hair. I couldn't wait to get dressed because the best was yet to come. After each bath I scrambled outside, stopped beneath the bathroom window and yelled "Pull the plug." At home we had city plumbing and sewer lines but, at Bud's the water poured down like heavy rain on the graveled ground under the house which was about 2 feet above ground level. This was a sight that held my undivided attention each time I bathed at my friends' farm. After dark I'd sometimes sit in Cordie's lap until she rocked me to sleep. There was no way Bud could rock me; with his potbelly, he had no lap. Other nights they allowed me to choose the records I wanted to play on the hand cranked console Victrola. Some of the records were as thick as a boot sole, all of them were scratchy, but the sounds of Enrico Caruso singing, John Phillip Sousa's band playing "The Stars and Stripes Forever," or Al Jolson warbling "Mammy" thrilled me almost as much as winding up the machine before playing each selection.

My memories of Bud and Cordie hold special places in my heart. They loved life and lived it to the fullest by sharing their unique way of life with others. Bud's resources were wiped out when King Cotton's fickle markets shifted; even though he died a broke and broken man, he will always be a prince in my storybook of memories.

BUT WHAT WOULD EMILY SAY?

By no stretch of one's imagination could our family bookshelf have been referred to as a library since it consisted of a total of only six memorable volumes. On the bookshelf beneath the telephone were a World Atlas, a one volume encyclopedia, a thick storybook featuring everything from Aesop's Fables to Mother Goose and Cinderella, a Webster's Dictionary, a King James version of the Bible and Emily Post's Blue Book of Etiquette. Second only to the Holy Scriptures in my household was Miss Post's guide regarding how one must comport herself in any given social situation. To my Mother, good manners were as imperative as clean fingernails, a maternal mandate Bubba and I were rarely allowed to bypass.

While it might seem strange that children in a small rural Texas community should be guided by such standards, it was not an unusual condition imposed on the youngsters in our town. At very early ages, in order to improve our manners, we were enrolled in classes conducted by older ladies who polished our behavioral patterns until we had learned to stand when elders entered the room, to speak only when spoken to and to use the proper fork when having dinner with family guests.

One of the skills we were challenged to become practiced in was the proper form of address. To most children this is a fairly easy art to master; not so in our society. While it was acceptable to address our parents' friends by their first names (Earl , Marie, Benny, Rolle, Louise, Estelle, Joe and Vira) this was totally unacceptable when speaking to or about friends of our grandparents. The older generation of merchants, businessmen and farmers were to be addressed as Mr. John, Mr. Gail, Mr. Jack and Mr. Carl. Of course professional men were referred to by their titles, hence Dr. Wootters, Dr. Stokes, Dr. Traylor and Judge Aldrich. Learning this protocol was not too complicated so we mastered these lessons quickly. What to call their wives was a different matter altogether. For some reason we were told to address one of the Mrs. Wootters' as "Miss Sue" and the other, "Miss Byrde, but neither as Mrs. Wootters. "Miss Cora" was the widow of Dr. Stokes, "Miss Ione" was actually Mrs. LeGory " and "Miss Genevieve" was Mr. Jack's own true love, but rarely called Mrs. Beasley. To complicate this even more, there were the maiden ladies of our local gentry who were truly misses: Miss Emma, Miss Sarah, and Miss Kathryn. The only married ladies I called "Mrs" anything were the wives of people who had moved to Crockett, newcomers without deeply planted roots in our community. I imagine this was our hamlet's clannish way of letting late arrivals know who had been around long enough to control or try to control the customs and mores of those at the top of the local social pecking order. I found it a strange custom, even though it was surely meant to be yet another way of showing one's respect.

For the ladies, the most important social happenings were afternoon teas. These were obligatory when announcing the engagement of one's daughter, to honor a daughter who had eloped with her Romeo, or to introduce the bride of a local swain who had just brought his new wife home. Much preparation was necessary for such a gathering. When Uncle George eloped with Aunt Helen, Mama shifted into high gear to plan the affair honoring her new daughter-in-law. Flowers had to be perfect to center the big round dining room table. Mama's instructions to the florist, as I recall, were that the arrangement should be placed in a epergne with blossoms cascading to the table top. Her best tablecloth, the one with embroidered edges around the delicately cut design, had to be laundered with great care, then sent to the dry cleaners to be pressed to perfection. Invitations must be written and mailed. Someone, usually Mrs. Keissling the church organist, would be invited to provide soft piano music and accompany the voice students singing such lovely tunes as " I Love You Truly" and "Because." Of course Mama had to determine in which order the members of the receiving line should stand and who would be honored to greet the guests, pour the tea and punch and serve the coffee. These designated matrons were known as the house party. I thought that a very odd term.

To add to the importance of the occasion, the hostess, the bride, the bride's mother and the house party were all attired in formal gowns, guests wore their very best outfits complete with their most fashionable millinery and appropriate gloves. Before the appointed time for the party, Mama's house was astir with the swishing of long dresses as the house party members dashed from one room to another, pausing graciously to compliment each other on their trappings. Once the guests arrived there was such a cackle of chatter it became difficult to hear what anyone person was talking about. The ladies loved it; the honoree was usually overwhelmed by it all.

The tea for Aunt Helen and later a similar one for Aunt Rebecca when she eloped with Uncle Ben, was apparently a success because the last guests left much later than the pre-announced ending hour.

Since none of Mother's brothers had a church wedding, Mama was spared the more rigorous undertaking of planning a tea for a bride-to-be. If the party were to honor a young lady planning a big church wedding, and all church weddings were referred as big, there was the dilemma of her colors. Once the upcoming marriage was scheduled, the bride chose the color her bridesmaids would wear at the wedding; for some reason this became plural and was referred to as "her colors." If her friends were to traipse down the aisle in pink every flower arrangement, invitation, corsage, bouquet, bag of rice, mint , punch and cake were required to be or be trimmed with this exact shade of pink. There seemed to be more discussion regarding this than almost anything else and was overshadowed only by the selection of the members of the wedding party.

The bridesmaids, usually high school friends blended with a smidgen of sorority sisters from college, ooh'ed and aah'ed over the dresses they would wear. This made no sense at all to me. How many weddings have you attended only to hear people say, both at the church and at the reception, that the bride was the most beautiful of the whole group? Naturally she was: it was planned that way from the very beginning. While the bridal gown was meticulously designed to accent the tiny waistline and youthfully slender arms of the bride, the attendant dresses were plain in design; lacking in detail. It seemed to me the dressmakers had purposefully meant for each bridesmaid to be as unattractive as Cinderella's stepsisters. They succeeded without exception; the dresses shouted "bridesmaid" so loudly they were never worn again.

While teas and weddings were the social highlights for which we were taught proper manners, there were still other lessons to be learned. After church many families enjoyed Sunday dinner at the Crockett Hotel where Alta Cornelius served not only the best food in town, but also the best black bottom pie imaginable. Unfortunately, because the services at the Baptist Church usually lasted longer, the Methodist and Presbyterian families were finishing their salads by the time we arrived. Our clan had to wait in the lobby until a table became available almost every week. For those of us who were eager to eat this was a real hardship; not so for Mother and Mama. They passed the time visiting with Miss Essie, Miss Florence and the other late arriving Baptists relishing each account of a recent shopping trip to Houston or the latest glories of their rose gardens.

When we were finally seated in the dining room there were more rules to be remembered; your napkin, cloth of course, must be placed in your lap not tucked in your collar; rolls belonged on the bread plate with the butter, not on your dinner plate; and above all, be sure to use the proper fork for each course. As the other towns folk finished their meals they stopped by our table to pass pleasantries with us. Gentlemen stood as a matter of courtesy on such occasions; this rule most assuredly included every young boy past toddler age. This friendliness often resulted in Poppa, Daddy and even Bubba, bouncing up and down like puppets on a string. As a consequence of their gallantry, the men and boys frequently dined on cold entrees, lukewarm potatoes and vegetables and melted desserts. Not once, however, did I hear a protest from them because they were displaying the genteel behavior of true gentlemen.

Additional polishing of our manners was provided by the various music teachers in our limited world. Mrs. Woodson, who everyone called Miss Maggie, Mrs. Keissling and Mrs. von Doenhoff suffered us through the scales until we were competent enough to perform in their annual recitals. Attendance was mandatory for parents and grandparents, but only the most doting aunts and uncles endured these lengthy affairs. Aunt Dot and Uncle Collin always came to mine and no matter if I had played only "Twinkle, Twinkle Little Star," Aunt Dot had a little gift to commemorate my accomplishments. Even though I had little or no talent for playing the piano, I took lessons for years; acquiring the skill was simply one of the things young ladies were expected to do. Taking lessons from "Miss Albertine, " a.k.a. Mrs. von Doenhoff proved to be an unforgettable experience. Although she was a Crockett native she had become an accomplished concert pianist in New York City and had married a composer. After the death of her husband, she returned home, ultimately to teach music to local children. Most of the time I arrived at the beautiful old gingerbread home of her parents a little early, not only because my music teacher had an aversion to tardiness, but also because of an intriguing set of books in the front hallway where I waited for my lesson.

These books, very thin gold edged pages bound in soft leather, were the entire works of William Shakespeare. I was in the seventh grade when I first discovered these treasures and looked forward to reading them almost more than taking my lessons. We had not been introduced to Shakespearean plays in our English classes at that time, so I don't know why I found them so fascinating, perhaps it was the difficulty I had understanding why people spoke in such a peculiar manner.

Teaching must have been an excruciating experience for one so talented to endure, especially when working with inept students like me. Miss Albertine did not allow her students to play popular music; hers was a strict and steady diet of Beethoven, Bach and Brahms. Once I managed the memorization and performance of some of these masters I just might be given the opportunity of selecting something as modern and difficult as a Gershwin prelude. At several points during my musical exposure Miss Albertine came close to scaring the Beethoven right out of me when it was obvious I had failed to practice. She could be very intimidating as she exclaimed, rather harshly, how I was wasting both her time and my parents' money by not taking my music more seriously.

Thanks to her persistence I learned a true appreciation of classical music, even though I had little aptitude for performing it.   For this gift, I shall be everlastingly grateful.

TEACHER, TEACHER

Pressure of achievement was not as important in my early school years as it is now. Only a few high school graduates each year aspired to college educations; most of those who did intended to become doctors, lawyers or teachers. Our parents were very concerned with our education, not because of the degrees we would earn, but because they wanted us to live useful lives. If we made good grades we were praised and congratulated; if we got poor marks in deportment, we were punished when report cards came out; if we got in trouble at school, we were in twice as much trouble when we got home. Parents supported the schools and the teachers. Every child realized quickly to take the business of learning seriously.

What a sad contrast this is to the indifference many parents show to public schools today. At least part of the change in attitudes regarding schools and teachers is due to the fact that teachers are no longer allowed to be educational tyrants they once were. Don't misunderstand, my teachers were not child abusers who beat knowledge into our heads but, they were very much in charge. Those who dared to question their authority soon found out who was on command of the classroom and rarely questioned it again. Despite their indubitable dominance over us we learned to love and to respect our teachers.

There were two buildings on the school grounds in Crockett; the high school and the grammar school. Later grammar school became known as elementary school, a junior high was initiated and high school was reduced to three years instead of four. These buildings and the campuses around them occupied all of a seven acre city block, except for the lots taken up the Methodist Church and the old Adams' family home.

My first day at school was anticipated for months; when the day finally arrived I was ready and eager to go. The three story red brick school offered little opportunity for personal inspection however, for the first floor was devoted exclusively to the first three grades. We were rarely allowed to venture beyond the limits proscribed our classes. The second floor was set aside for grades four and five, the auditorium, principal's office and teachers' lounge. Following the predictable sequence, only the sixth, seventh and eighth grade students were housed on the top floor. I've been told the reason high school is so designated is due to the fact that as children progressed, the older ones were trained in rooms higher than the others. If this is true, it was certainly well illustrated in our school.

All classrooms were very much like, at least one wall was all windows so tall shades had to be pulled up from the middle to cover their upper portions. Blackboards covered two walls and the other was a one bulletin board the teacher changed monthly. In the rooms assigned to the lower grades each blackboard was topped with printed capital and lower case examples of every letter of the alphabet; the upper grades' boards had alphabet written in script. Desks were aligned in straight rows, each permanently secured to the dark heavily oiled wooden floors with oversized screws. Our desks were always the same style although their sizes changed ,as did ours, when we moved up in the grades. They were quite different from those used today. Iron brackets, not unlike those of treadle operated sewing machines, supported the writing surface of one desk and the folding seat of the one in front of it. Beneath the desk top was a shelf on which we stored our books, tablets, paper and smaller supplies, which were always kept in cigar boxes. On the right of each desktop was hole to be used for your ink bottle and across the upper section, a groove to keep pencils from rolling to the floor. We were instructed to wrap our textbooks with book covers and advised not to write on the desks. Apparently this was one teachers' order disobeyed with great frequency. I never remember being assigned a desk without names and drawings scribbled all over it.

One of the skills we were taught was called penmanship. I felt very important the first time my school supply list included a pen staff, pen points and a bottle of washable blue ink. I never understood why it was called washable ink because ink spots on my clothes never seemed to disappear. Oh, it was washable for sure, because no matter how many times school clothes were washed, the ink always survived to remind you of your classroom mistake.

In Mrs. Carpenter's third grade class, one the highlights was to practice row after row of push-pulls and oval-ovals until we mastered writing with a pen. Unfortunately not all my efforts were neat due either to blobs of ink, or to the condition of the pen point. One must understand in this day of the ballpoint that five for a dime pen points were very often most stubborn objects. If they had not been held over a flame to roughen their surfaces, they would hold ink; if they had too much pressure applied to them, they would split right up the middle making writing an impossibility until another could be prepared properly; if they were handled with an unsteady hand or a jerking motion, they would spit unsightly hieroglyphics in the middle of an otherwise perfectly written sentence. No matter how I tried I never seemed to master penmanship well enough to make the beautifully formed letter Mrs. Carpenter wrote on the blackboard.

It was a thrill, as well as a major accomplishment, to get my first fountain pen. This challenged us to learn still another skill. Filling a fountain pen was an adult-like achievement denoting our steady progress toward maturity. The ink bottles had a small ink well near the top it. These could only be filled with the precious fluid by tilting the bottle to one side at the correct angle. We learned to make sure the cap was screwed on firmly before we attempted this replenishment, but not before most of us had managed to spill a new bottle of ink on everything within splashing distance. While fountain pens were less difficult to master than pen points, they were certainly not without hazards. If you pulled the lever too hard when filling it, it could burst the rubber tube inside. Somehow this was never detected until ink oozed out of the cylinder covering my fingers and notebook paper with smudges. In addition to this disappointment, there was the risk of being squirted by a mischievous classmate when the teacher had her back to the class. The art of ink squirting required more finesse than paper wad throwing and gave birth to the broadest range of creative excuses one could imagine.

Although I use ball point pens today, I still prefer the appearance of a letter written with a fountain pen. Years of note taking and sloppy habits have caused my penmanship to deteriorate but, at least at one point in my life I did possess an almost acceptable handwriting style. It seems shameful to me that penmanship is no longer emphasized in our schools, for it is one of the few totally personalized traits remaining in our increasingly impersonal society.

Letters, legal documents and business records written by my great grandparents reveal beautifully formed letters written with undeniable pride; those of my grandparents divulge less attention to the formation of letters and flourishes. The written records of my parents disclose a more hurried manner; mine, for the most part, typed with a jumbled signature almost illegibly scratched across the bottom. Is it possible that future generations will use computer screens to record their thoughts and never really learn to write as I did? What a pity.

I first experienced having a male teacher in the fifth grade. When Mr. Mason entered the room we knew he meant for us to listen and learn; he would tolerate no nonsense. He taught us tricks using numbers and developed rhymes that helped us learn multiplication tables. His teaching style made arithmetic interesting and fun, which may well account for the fact it was later one of my better subjects. For those of my classmates who did not find his numerical drilling as much fun as I, he was perceived as a real task master. Despite his authoritative manner, Mr. Mason managed to incorporate some humor into almost every day's class in such a way we laughed at his mistakes. I realized these mistakes were carefully planned but, he was very adept at getting and holding our attention. As we advanced to word problems he used his most polished presentation of these opportunities. "If Sam has three apples, Mary has four pears and Tom has five oranges, what do we have?" He literally rolled out the red carpet for the class wise guy to respond, "fruit salad."

Painstakingly worded questions regarding trains speeding in opposite directions inevitably resulted in responses of "train wreck," or "head on collision." About one subject, however, he had no sense of humor. He expounded his theory that fingers were made for many uses-- holding things, pointing, playing the piano and shooting marbles, but one purpose for which they were never to be used was counting. Heaven help the misguided schoolchild caught counting on his fingers. Some force needed to protect them because anyone seen counting on his fingers was sure to get his hands slapped by Mr. Mason's thick wooden ruler. Our attention span was lengthened considerably after a couple of encounters with his measuring stick.   Willingly or reluctantly, we learned arithmetic well under his tutelage.

Introduction to geography and history opened our eyes to the many wonders outside our isolated small town.

In Mrs. Barbee's class we studied big maps which rolled up above the blackboards when not in use. Maps became more and more personal to us during the war as each student was allowed to place a sticker on them to indicate where family members were, or in many case, where we assumed they were if they were in combat zones. Before we got to that part of our studies, we were introduced to the Tigris and Euphrates rivers as the cradles of civilizations. We studied the glories of Egypt, the conquests of the Holy Roman Empire and the development of the British Empire. All of us acquired a yearning to travel to each country we saw through the eyes of our teacher . We had no slide projectors or movie equipment so the burden of stimulating our young imaginations laid heavily upon the teacher's ability to describe life styles, landscapes and customs of the faraway lands we studied.

One of the most useful aids educators had was the WEEKLY READER newspaper not only because of its content, but also because we looked forward to getting it with such eagerness. It was another milestone in our educational progress to have a newspaper of our own. As our parents read stories of the bombing of Britain, we learned about Westminster Abbey and saw pictures of London's children boarding trains bound for the safety of the English countryside. As the grown ups' news focused on Paris, we discovered the Gothic beauty of Notre Dame cathedral with its majestic flying buttresses and grotesque gargoyles.

To make our geography lessons still more personal we were encouraged to write a pen pal in another English speaking country. Mine lived in Manchester, England and although I only remember her first name was Elizabeth, I do recall the contents of her letters. I found it odd that our Santa Claus was referred to as Father Christmas by my friend. Even though I tried to explain to her that Yankees were people who lived in the northern part of our country and Southerners lived in my home town, she insisted upon calling every American a Yank. We exchanged picture post cards as I tried time and again to explain to her that Texans didn't ride horses to work and wear six shooters; she attempted to explain the importance of tea time to me. My distant friend and I corresponded for two years. I never got a picture of her, but I felt I knew her well. Do children still have pen pals, or do they just chat on the Internet?

When Mrs. King joined the faculty none of us knew what to expect. The older kids could not tell us what she was like because she was new to the school. She was tall, large-framed woman who wore her hair in a bun and possessed the liveliest, most twinkling eyes and most beautiful smile of all our teachers. Although I'm sure she taught other subjects I remember her art classes best. Under her sharp eyes and guidance we learned to paint posters using tempera paint, not straight of out the jars but by blending first one, then another until we created the exact shade and tone our childish imaginations required. We learned to paint letters with brushes quite different from those we'd used with watercolors. Our Christmas cards could be done with fancy letters printed with India ink and pen points with rounded or blunt edges, each of which was used for different characters. It was in her class we learned how to make wood block prints and to identify the works of great masters.

While she made all those things important, the most valuable lessons I learned from Mrs. King had nothing to do with art. Some of the children attending our school were from less fortunate families; it was not uncommon for these youngsters to come to school barefoot because they had no shoes. When one of my classmates ridiculed such a child everything came to a halt. Mrs. King ordered us to return to our seats and proceeded to teach us a lesson in compassion and understanding with all the fervor of a crusader. By the time she was through, we realized how lucky we were and how very unkind we had been to belittle someone who was different.

Of all the disciplinarians in our school Mrs. Sallas was the most feared at first; the most respected later. While none of the instructors allowed much nonsense in their classes, we sensed she would endure less than anyone else. She was tall, gray-haired woman, the widowed mother of two grown sons. Earlier in life she had goiter surgery which had afflicted her with a deep raspy quality to her voice unlike any other I'd heard. This tonal distinction only added greater authority to her presence. Mrs. Sallas was my eighth grade teacher in reading and spelling. Beyond our assigned textbook reading, we were expected to read such classics as Black Beauty, Little Women, Tom Sawyer and The Christmas Carol for book reports. Before she would accept our written book reports, we were required to prepare detailed outlines of what we had read. Those things were impossible to master to her standards.

The first was too detailed; the next, too sketchy. We drew up outlines several times before we finally got her approval; by then, we had learned to separate important information from secondary points, her goal for us from the beginning.

She contended one could be well read and well educated only if he took time to develop a good vocabulary. To help us achieve this goal, Mrs. Sallas' spelling classes were expanded not only to include the correct spelling of a word but, also to encompass the proper definitions as well. These classes became legend in our school. If you missed the definition of one word, if you missed the spelling by just one letter you stayed after school until you got it right. Her after school sessions were as full as regular classes but, we all learned how to spell, pronounce and define every word on her list before the year was over. I often judge a book by the author's use of the English language. If it introduces me to a word with which I'm not familiar I look it up in the dictionary until I've learned to spell it, pronounce it and define it. Thank you, Mrs. Sallas.

English grammar was the dominion of Mrs. Wootters, though we never called her by that name. To us, she was Miss Hattie. Even though she was petite, immaculately groomed and very proper, she left no doubt the class was under her jurisdiction. Occasionally, when we became bored by the conjugation of a verb and tended to be restless and inattentive, she would drum her fingers on the desk with the rapidity of machine gun fire. This signaled us to sit up straight and pay attention with the same air of a command one might hear from the lips of a drill sergeant. Following her wordless command Miss Hattie lowered her voice until at times we almost had to lean forward to hear what she was saying.

She was an extremely talented musician who used these talents to control students; she utilized pianissimo techniques to get our attention with much finesse. It worked well. She was the teacher who taught us to think straight, to write good paragraphs, to use our vocabularies properly and to express our ideas effectively without becoming verbose. My writing skill were fine tuned by high school instructors and college professors however, most of the credit for my being able to express myself in writing must be attributed to Miss Hattie. She laid the foundation for what has been one of the most meaningful and fulfilling crafts I've ever acquired.

Miss Hattie provided us with a bonus, for in addition to English, she also taught music appreciation. At times she the piano while we sang "Erie Canal," and "Skip to My Lou" with the gusto only children possess. At times she played records of symphonic music for us. The symphonies challenged us to identify which instruments were being played and where each section was located on the stage. Obtaining this knowledge enabled me to enjoy a solitary Sunday afternoon pastime. While the adults indulged in their traditional afternoon coffee and conversations at my grandparents', I went to the front bedroom, tuned the radio to the Longine Symphonette program and, with pencil in hand, directed each performance. I led every section through all the largos, pianissimos and crescendos as though I were Toscanni himself. My premiere performances were the rousing William Tell Overture and the 1812 Overture, for which I took my most appreciated pretend bows. Miss Hattie provided with a pleasure much greater than she ever imagined; even today I still hold symphonic music as a favorite diversion.

If you didn't have teachers like the ones I've describe, I pity you. They no longer exist for the number of reasons; the main one of which I suspect is based on our fast-food, instant gratification society. I don't believe the education of a child should be rushed. It is not a drive-through, pick me up quick type situation many parents seem to expect; nor is it a way to squander time until maturity is reached and megabucks can be earned performing some athletic prowess. Education, like childhood, should be appreciated for what it was meant to be: a period of exploration. Thankfully I was allowed, indeed encouraged, to explore and to enjoy this to the fullest.

HE WAS EVERYBODY'S BROTHER

In my basic Bible-belt upbringing it was natural that one of the men influencing my young life was the minister of the First Baptist Church. It was not until I was much more mature that I realized why it was named the "First" Baptist Church. Southern Baptists, and I was always told there was a great distinction to being a Southern Baptist rather than just a garden variety Baptist , had a habit of disagreeing with the preacher. If a hard-headed minister refused to yield to the congregation's demands, the rejected faction would simply split off and start their own church. Since each Southern Baptist church was an autonomous organization without the control of bishops, dioceses or synods, the members of the church could, and indeed did, determine the criteria regarding how the congregation was to be governed. Uncle Collin, in a rare mood following a deacon's meeting, made the statement that the reason there were so many Baptists was because they were like cats, dividing frequently and multiplying quickly. There must have been some degree of truth to his statement; there are now four or five Baptist churches in the town I love so dearly.

The pastor of our church was Rev. Albert Sidney Lee. His wife called him Sid, but to everyone else in town, he was Brother Lee. As a child I didn't understand why a man the age of my grandfather should be call Brother, but the moniker stayed with him until the day he died. I never knew what his educational background was because Baptist ministers in those days were "called" to serve the Lord and many of them had little, if any, formal training as was required by other denominations. I do recall that Mrs. Lee, when she was told she had done something unbecoming to a preacher's wife, would reply, "I didn't marry a preacher. I married a barber." This was amusing to me because Brother Lee had the tiniest fringe of hair beginning with thin sideburns inching around his ears all the way to a monumental two or three inches of hair above the nape of his neck. Above these precious locks shone the glassy, almost polished looking bald head of the man who was so dear to so many. Beneath this tonsorial disaster was a radiant face exuding all that was right with world, even when all around him griped and were fault-finding with nearly everything.

He was a gentle man, a man's man, a lover of children, a man totally devoted to his faith, his God and his church. For all his gentleness, however, he delivered sermons with such resounding authority his congregation was awed by his messages. He had a booming voice when preaching, not the kind of shouting and emotionalism we now associate with TV evangelists, but one filled with devout conviction in what he was discussing was what his flock needed to hear and hear well each Sunday morning. His mere appearance filled my heart with happiness; he looked in many ways like the Santa Claus in my story books, without the beard of course. When he spoke of Moses I almost expected him to part the Red Sea; at Easter I visualized him having stood by the empty tomb declaring reverently, "He is risen!"

Our church was a rather reserved flock by most Baptist standards. It was the custom that when a youngster reached the age of twelve, the age of accountability it was called, it was time for he or she to join the church and be baptized. My twelfth birthday came and went without my answering the invitation to join the church. Thankfully my parents did not push my decision, but instead allowed me to take my own time to determine if I were ready to become a member. I sat with my parents and grandparents in the same pew every Sunday and heard all the reasons one should aspire to become a Christian. I had no argument with any of the rationale but, until I could have a real solemn talk with Brother Lee about what it all meant, I could not make that long walk down the aisle to proclaim to God and everyone present I wished to be a Christian. My chats with him made my decision easy and in a few weeks I walked down the aisle with conviction and determination.

After the war began Brother Lee became more and more a counselor to families of those who fought, were wounded and died for our freedom. Soon the congregation was interspersed with khaki Army uniforms, bell bottom blue Navy issue, dress gabardines worn by Army officers and green dress uniforms sported by Marines. Every serviceman wanted to visit his church when home of leave, and none left without a copy of the 91st Psalm given them by the pastor.

I will say of the Lord, He is my refuge and my fortress; my God, in Him will I trust.... Thou shalt not be afraid for the terror by night nor for the arrow that flieth by day...... A thousand shall fall at thy side and ten thousand at thy right hand, but it shall no come nigh thee.....there shall no evil befall thee; I will be with him in trouble, I will deliver him

He corresponded with servicemen who were members of his congregation as well as many who were not, and announced their latest news from his pulpit before he led us in united prayer for their safe return. He was the first to respond to a need for help; the last to abandon hope for those who were missing in action; the most comforting to the families of those who did not return.

Our church building burned on a cold December Sunday shortly after the War ended. It was the most spectacular fire our little town had ever seen. I felt an emptiness as its huge dome caved in and the slightly out of tune pipe organ groaned one last sigh, as if to say goodbye. Numbers of people of all faiths stood across the street and wept as the magnificent old red brick building continued to burn. We watched the gentle handsome stained glass faces of Jesus and the Disciples melt in the unbearable heat. It was a dark night in Crockett even though the sky blistered with flames for hours before the blazes were diminished to a massive heap of glowing embers. It was this type of adversity which brought our citizenry together.

The following day funds were started to rebuild the church, much of it from members of other churches. A generous member of the Methodist board of elders donated all the pews for the new church in honor of Brother Lee. That started an avalanche of monies from all over the county. There was even a sizable donation from the town's only avowed agnostic and many from former servicemen Brother Lee had comforted through the mail for the duration of the War. I sensed these gifts were monuments both to God and to a man who had proven his love for the entire community. No wonder everyone called him brother.

My Favorite Fellows

My childhood memories are filled with thoughts of the men I loved even before I was old enough to realize much of my life would be centered around males. There were any number of men in my young life; family members, gas station owners, businessmen, clergymen, farmers and teachers. Their memories are as alive in me as headlines in today's newspapers.

The businessmen in Crockett were unusually distinguished by small town standards. Most of them were very neatly attired; good grooming seemed to be their trademark. As a rule these gentlemen made their bank deposits at the same hour each day. Following their transactions with bankers, they met to discuss civic and business news with their friends. These impromptu meetings stemmed serious discussions as well as good hearted joking as they stood on the sidewalk in front of Millar and Berry's men's store.

No doubt, people driving through town wondered who the group of suit-clad men were. As they talked, some would hang their thumbs in vest pockets, others would toy with a fraternity or civic club medal hanging from a watch chain; some simply jammed their hands in the pockets of their trousers; but each man had a unique posture from which he set forth his best ideas for increasing business, improving the city or bettering the local school system.

Among this group of locally influential men was a most important man in my life, my grandfather Ben Satterwhite. He was a self educated man whose formal schooling ended with the third grade. He wasn't a tall man, yet he wasn't what one would describe as a man of slight build either. His eyes sparkled with his singular personality, the type which caused him to laugh wholeheartedly at someone's funny story; the kind which afforded him utter delight when one of his children or grandchildren answered one of his many riddles with an unexpected retort; the sort he used to effectively nudge friends into taking a firm stand on a civic matter he supported, then convince them it had been their idea from the start.

He lived for faith and his family and was extremely devoted to both. Poppa was his happiest when surrounded by his family, and I do mean surrounded, for my grandparents had six children and at the time of his death, there were twelve grandchildren and three great-grandchildren.

Nothing delighted him more than having his brood around the big round dining table on Sundays and holidays. He assigned each member of the family a seat at the table and after he returned thanks for the meal, carefully carved the meat for the main course and urged everyone to enjoy the meal. As soon as we finished the meal Poppa left the table to be joined by the men in the sitting room. They discussed business, hunting, church affair or any of the many other interests they shared. These 'bull sessions," as he called them , only made the clan more close knit. As busy as he was with all his activities, my grandfather was never too busy to spend time with his first granddaughter; I loved having his undivided attention.

The first time I remember going swimming was with Poppa. We went to the lake, Crockett's rustic version of a country club, where the bottom had been cleared of debris and sand hauled in to make a safe, attractive swimming area. Around this swimming hole was an L shaped wooden pier, one side of which was outfitted with benches for onlookers to oversee young swimmers, near the front of the pier a spring board and diving tower for the amusement of adults and older accomplished swimmers. A rough cedar building with wide steps leading into the water supplied us with stalls in which to change into our bathing attire. Children today would laugh at the manner my grandfather dressed for swimming. He wore baggy swim trunks into which was tucked the tail of a sleeveless knit shirt. To him, this was the only proper attire a gentleman should wear for water sports. My uncles wore only trunks, as did most of the younger generation, but Poppa remained faithful to his aquatic costume. Only after he had buckled me into a bright orange life jacket did he take me in his arms and wade into the waist deep water. When he turned me loose, I felt abandoned, but his reassuring word, as well as the life jacket, kept me afloat. I realized he was never more than a step away. His presence made the lake not quite so big; the water not so deep and eventually I overcame my fear of water and learned to swim.

Poppa's modesty once got me in big trouble; he used the incident to teach me a valuable lesson about respecting others' privacy. One of his priorities was to keep his body fit, if for no other reason than to be at his peak when hunting season rolled around. To accomplish this goal, he exercised to music played on thick records he put on the Victrola; the music sounded like the bands I'd heard at the Texas Centennial parade. Once the music started, he placed thick cards on the floor in front of him and emulated the posture of the man on them until he had done a prescribed number of each exercise. The man on the cards looked like pictures of John L. Sullivan, for his cardboard instructor wore tights and sported a classic handlebar mustache. Each placard showed the man in several positions one should master in order to keep fit. While it was acceptable for me to see his set of cards, it was quite another matter for me to sneak into the bedroom to watch Poppa do his fitness routine.

He spotted me in the doorway and told it was not proper for a young lady to see her grandfather attired only in the BVDs; hurriedly pulled on his bathrobe, grabbed my arm and sat me in a chair; expounded on his views regarding the invasion of someone's privacy. Since it was rare for him to scold me, it became a lesson I learned quickly and have never forgotten. Although this home was open to all, Poppa valued his private time and space, a trait not difficult to understand in a man who was one of a dozen children and the father of six.

One of his private places was a cedar wardrobe, which today would be described as a rustic armoire. One side provided space for his suits, consistently dark woolen ones for winter and seersucker for summer, jackets and trousers; the other, drawers for shirts, socks and underwear. As long as he lived, I never remember this piece being unlocked in his absence. On rare special occasions he allowed me to look in "chiffarobe," as he called it. He shared his amazing possessions with me. The little wooden box he explained, was used to attract wild turkeys when he was hunting. When he demonstrated his skill with the apparatus he said that was how turkeys sounded in the wild. Another fascinating gadget was his duck call which sounded like the ducks we'd heard at the lake. But of all his private treasures, the one I found most intriguing was a contrivance to sharpen razor blades. He locked a dulled blade in place, turned the handle a few times and suddenly had a nice, sharp blade to be used longer than its maker had intended. No doubt, razor blade manufacturers played a big role in keeping this gadget a secret, for his was the only one I ever saw during my formative years and I have yet to see another.

Adjacent to his wardrobe, Poppa had a steel gun case; always locked and strictly off-limits even to my uncles. He was a real sportsman; a crack shot who used his skill for game in quail, dove, duck, turkey and deer season. Out of season he stayed in practice by shooting skeet. I was awed by his preciseness when I saw him break clay pigeons into thousands of tiny pieces almost as quickly as they were released from the skeet trap. His office was filled with mounted heads of multi-pointed deer whose eyes stared down glaringly upon all who wished to transact business with him.

The war changed my grandfather; he became quieter than usual after three sons and a grandson went away to serve their country. For the first time in my memory, Poppa smoked cigarettes, a habit he never became adept at because he didn't inhale and held the slender cylinders of tobacco between his thumb and middle finger in a most awkward manner. Most of his smoking, if you could call it that, was done as he listened to the radio reports of the mellow-toned Edward R. Murrow, or the rapid clipped words of H.V. Kalthenborn. Each day, he was mesmerized by their accounts of American soldiers, their gains, and losses and our country's status in winning the war.

In 1941 Germany had invaded Russia and lay siege to Leningrad. President Roosevelt called for a Lend Lease program to aid Britain. As these events unfolded, our family became more and more concerned regarding the future. Their anxiety increased throughout the year, yet we were reassured by our leaders we would not become a part of the political strife taking place in Europe.

On December 7, 1941 our nation's worst nightmare became reality when the Japanese crippled the entire U.S. fleet with their sneak attack on Pearl Harbor. The next day President Roosevelt asked Congress to declare was on Japan. Within days Germany and Italy declared war on our country and we were deeply involved in the most wide spread war of the century.

Prior to these tragic times, Poppa had a little pet ditty he repeated when it was time to get hopping. He would say "Toop-de-da-roop" to a Skip to My Lou cadence when he was about the business of overseeing his grandchildren play a game or let the family know it was time to step lively to join in a special treat. Throughout the dark earlier days of the worldwide conflict ,he seldom Toop-de-da-rooped and when he did, it was not with his former sense of pleasure. I missed the frequency of his personal ditty and was thrilled to hear it more often as time passed and the war news became more encouraging.

I hope all children look upon someone dear to them with the same admiration I had for Poppa. He taught me many valuable lessons, sometimes planned, sometimes by just setting an example.

Naturally, the other man greatly influencing my life was my Daddy, a man who admired my grandfather as much as I did. Daddy, an easygoing, level headed man, found humor in almost any situation. His humor included amusing incidents which caused you to chuckle quietly rather than laugh with side bursting guffaw. His magnetic personality made him perfectly suited for his job as a salesman, for he liked everyone and most folks returned his friendship. During my young years, Daddy was a fisherman who frequently camped out on the river banks or lake with friends. Few things provided him more pleasure than bringing home a string of fish, unless it was packing for yet another excursion. His camping apparatus was fairly simple, rather primitive by comparison to the elaborate fishing equipment of today. He and Uncle Collin, his favorite fishing partner, would load their jointly owned wooden boat on top of the car, fill it with cots, old quilts, mosquito netting, tackle boxes and minnow seines, pack the car with enough food for a small army and leave for whatever was their current hot spot. More often then not, the two dedicated anglers returned with far more insect bites than fish; nevertheless, they returned happy, relaxed and ready for another few weeks of work.

Their work, selling groceries to small town merchants, was tiring, yet enjoyable to them. Often Daddy would sell enough flour or starch to win a premium for his outstanding sales; which accounted for mother having eight brand new wool blankets to be used on the three beds in our house. There were other awards I enjoyed such as a set of twelve children's books, but Daddy enjoyed the 22 rifle and endless quantity of fishing lures he accumulated much more.

During the summer months Daddy would take me to work with him at least two or three days. It was on these trips I learned about old-fashioned general stores as I observed the businesses and their friendly owners. While each store had its own personality, they were all very much alike. Almost without exception in front of the store were hand pump style gasoline pumps and several kerosene tanks with funny looking handles from which the merchant dispensed kerosene for the lamps which lighted rural homes of the day. The interior had such awesome decor as horse collars and No. 3 wash tubs hanging from the exposed rafters, a bulky scale for weighing sacks of feed and grain for farm stock and one glass enclosed display case filled with pink peanut patty candy, Luden cough drops, Double Bubble gum,

Red Man chewing tobacco, Prince Albert pipe tobacco, cigarette papers, Bull Durham tobacco, and a few Camel cigarettes, thread, needles, buttons and the omnipresent King Edward cigar box filled with the storekeeper's accounts receivable records.

It was hard to imagine anything these stores didn't have. You could buy straw hats, piece goods, socks, work gloves, pots and pans, livestock medicine, patent medicines, tops, kites, canned goods, meats, cheese, staples, school supplies, seed, rope, dishes, diapers, baby potties, kerosene lamps and cane bottomed rocking chairs all under the same roof.

There was usually a small building nearby containing huge blocks of ice; still another held plows and farming tools. For the simple needs of the community, this store had everything one could need or want. The atmosphere was one of relaxed, friendly companionship where it was almost impossible to feel anything but good will toward those who ran the store, those who shopped there or those who merely stopped for a chat on a rainy day to discuss how poorly his crops were and how good his neighbors' were growing.

My trips to Daddy to visit these stores were very enjoyable. While the men were attending to the business at hand I amused myself by trying on straw hats, weighing on the feed scales, climbing to the top of a stack of sacked feed or getting behind the counter where I pretended to be the store owner. Going shopping in such a store was a chance to visit with neighbors, to catch up on the news of which young man was courting the Jones girls, whose cow had a new calf and how much Old Man Smith wanted for the 12 acres of river bottom land he had for sale. It was a far cry from today's run up the aisle, grab it before they run out of it, check out and go shopping. Life moved at a slower pace then and people enjoyed themselves, though they had little materially since struggling through the Depression. They didn't have all the luxuries we now consider necessities, but they had something special. They had the belief that each day was filled with God's richest blessings which should be appreciated; such blessings as good health, normal children, loving husbands and wives, and faith in our fellow man. These values make me wish sometimes we could all return to the general stores I knew just long enough to take inventory of ourselves and to reevaluate our true purpose in life.

When Daddy was all dressed up, he wore his white linen suit and a sailor straw hat. There were many varieties of white suits in those days, but no matter which Daddy wore he always came out looking like a white bean pole. He was so thin I sometimes wondered how his body continued to hold up all six feet of him.

But, that was the fashion then so when Daddy got dressed for church or social functions Mother always thought him exceedingly handsome.

Daddy was by no means a fashion plate; at times this caused mild disagreements between my parents. One year in preparation for a big costume party, all their friends spent weeks preparing for the affair. Mother decided to go as Scarlett O'Hara. She searched through old, musty trunks in local attics before she found the one authentic Civil War period gown she wanted. She spent days coordinating her ensemble. In her search she had found a "perfect" outfit for Daddy, but he was much too tall to wear it. Mother was terribly disappointed but, as was customary, Daddy assured her everything would work out okay. He didn't shave for days; Mother was confident this would result in a gentlemanly beard. On the evening of the social affair, Daddy appeared in the most authentic looking hobo outfit not belonging to an actual knight of the road. He was mess! The regally attired Scarlett walked with the pride of a queen until she saw her escort. She vowed she would not go to the party with a tramp. Daddy just laughed, and they went to the party, where my beautiful Mother impressed everyone, but Daddy won first prize for best costume.

They were a happy couple who did things together, long before ladies magazines invented "togetherness." Each fall we had the joy of gathering the nuts from the six tremendous pecan trees in our yard. Most homes in Crockett had pecan trees in the yard thanks to the Chamber of Commerce, who offered homeowners the trees for small sums in an effort to beautify the town. They planted so many trees, Crockett became know as the city of 10,000 nut trees with a population of 5,000 nuts, at least that was the local joke. During the nut harvest Daddy climbed the trees, and jumped up and down on the limbs until all the nuts had fallen on tarpaulins he spread on the ground. Picking up all those nuts as a real task. The leaves that had fallen along with the pecans were raked into neat piles before Daddy moved on to job of thrashing the next tree. These leaves offered delightful pleasure to the neighborhood children; first for the thrill of leaping on the pile itself and then for a dry leaf fight, a thrill exceeded only by a feather pillow fight. The second time Daddy raked the leaves he touched a match to them immediately to end his labor intensive yard work, but he never scolded us for the mess we had made.

If you have surmised from my varied experiences that I loved and respected Daddy, then I have expressed my thoughts well. I loved him dearly. This didn't just happen, it was developed throughout years of listening to his wisdom and following his examples, especially where here was a principle involved. He was what some might call an All American guy; a friend might call a good Joe and what a loving daughter called her hero.

Mother and Daddy read the newspaper every evening. After the war started they poured over every article with even more interest. Daddy made the news come alive for me when he explained Admiral Nimitz, whose picture was in the paper, was the head of the entire Pacific fleet. He added, that I knew his parents. I did? Yes indeed, they owned the hotel in the hill country I had visited with my grandparents. I could hardly wait to tell the kids at school the next day that I knew the family of such an important man. When the president made a speech asking the world to protect the Four Freedoms, my Daddy explained what each of the freedoms represented in ways my childish mind could understand. Then the government initiated War Bonds, Daddy started giving me a dime each week to buy war stamps; when you got a book full of these, you could get a bond. The importance of this was explained to me as well. I am sure the reason so many events of the war years are embedded so vividly in my memory is that my parents gave me a real sense of history by reading the news to me.

The Role Models I Loved

Long before anyone ever heard of Women's Rights, there were the right women; the kind so rare today, the professional Mother who mellows into the experienced grandmother. One of our modern day tragedies is that many children never have the opportunity to develop a warm, over the years relationship with their grandmothers because of mobility, two-career or single parent families.

Even though most of my contemporaries had a similar relationship with their grandmother, I felt luckier than most because my grandmother was Mama Charm. She was the only daughter in a family of five who spend much of their young lives in a local boarding house bearing the name of my great grandparents: The Aldrich House. Mama told little of what life was like back then; except at Christmas when she made stuffed dates, a family tradition originated in Granny's boarding house kitchen.

I've seen only one picture of my grandmother when she was young, I'd say about 13 years old. She had a cute little turned up nose with a mass of dark curls surrounding her round face and an ever so slight twinkle in her eyes. She told me this picture was taken on a trip to Galveston, but the photograph was in no way the highlight of her trip. According to her, on this excursion she tasted her first banana, a fruit she found so delicious she became ill from eating too many. There were other pictures she shared with me. Pictures of my younger grandparents and friends on a trip to Mobile, Alabama and more formal snaps of the membership of the ladies club to which she belonged. Somehow, while all the photographs resembled Mama, it was difficult for me to imagine her as she had been in the past. Today, when everyone seems so preoccupied with the idea of eternal youth, running, fat-free diets and "thin is beautiful," it is almost impossible to believe that a snowy haired lady with six children, who was five feet tall and half as wide was called "cute," but that's precisely what she was.

Her personality was endearing. Her laugh announced to the whole of her small world that life itself was beautiful. Mama's basic attire was always the same, a bit more formal for church and parties, but the same nevertheless. In the fall and winter, she wore dark dresses with tiny pearl buttons and lace collars and cuffs; in the warmer weather, her dresses were pastel prints but the rest remained unchanged. Her weekday wardrobe was completed with either black or navy shoes; open toed, laced tightly around her tiny size five feet and always with what she called a sensible heel.

On Sundays Mama topped her ensembles with big picture hats, usually adorned with flowers, ostrich plumes, colorful feathers or pearls stylishly entwined with soft netting or delicate lace around the hat band. The same milliner made her custom designed hats every year. Her choice of toppers became her trademark in local society; in my eyes, nobody else in the world looked as beautiful in a hat as Mama did.

Just as the kitchen door was always open, so was Mama's heart. She was one of those rare individuals who took appropriate steps to help a young man working at the gas station across the street to earn his college tuition. Mama knew how little money he was making so she insisted he eat his noon meal with her family every day. For most people this would have seemed like charity and would not have been accepted; from Mama, it was hospitality and warmth offered through love and accepted in the same manner.

During the war it was commonplace for convoys of Army trucks to come past my grandparents' house as troops transferred from a dry, rocky, God forsaken camp in Texas to a wet, swampy, equally as forsaken base in Louisiana. Since ours was the last cross street in town, these convoys would often stop nearby. Travel weary young soldiers would climb down from the truck to stretch their legs and take a half hour break. Whenever this happened, Mama went into action. Rationing or no rationing, she would make lemonade with real sugar, calling on me to serve the cool drinks to the soldiers. In no time at all I had a card table set up near an aged hickory tree facing the highway and yelled, "Ice cold lemonade. Come and get it!" While the thirsty GI's enjoyed their refreshments Mama brought out other goodies; cookies, fresh fruit and candy. Occasionally a GI would offer to pay for the lemonade but I knew if I took one red cent I'd be in big trouble with Mama. Mr. Lawson, owner of the gas station across the street, always knew when they were coming because army scouts tipped him off a day or two in advance. He always let Mama know when her "boys" were coming. She got up at the break of day to bake cookies and make sandwiches for the servicemen who were so far from home. It was her way to make their tiresome, uncomfortable trip a little bit more bearable by reminding them of the homes they'd left behind.

Mama was most adorable when she got upset about something I use the term "upset' because I never recall seeing Mama angry. When she had done something foolish, her favorite saying was , "Blessed God, what a dumb thing to do." If she was perturbed by her children or grandchildren, she would protrude her bottom lip and puff at the curly wisps of baby fine hair circling her face until the tiny ringlets blew in every direction. She often played the piano and when we heard her playing the same ragtime tune over and over and louder and louder, we knew she was upset with Poppa.

Often on summer afternoons Mother and some neighborhood ladies met on the front porch to visit with Mama. While there are front porches all over the world, this was a front porch with a capital P, for it wrapped around half the house. The house was a massive structure which I was told was planned to be a two-story until Mama declared she had no intention of climbing stairs everyday to keep up with all those children. At this point Poppa had the builder change the plans, building a dormitory type room across the back of the house for the boys to share. Mama's change in plans accounted for the poorly placed hallway in the center of the house; the space was originally intended to be the stairway. At an earlier time, the house was painted green with darker green trim, but I never remember it being any color but white. The porch had brick steps on three sides; its floor was painted gunmetal gray. For guests' comfort an assortment of chairs and the traditional porch swing were on hand, but the most important chair of all was Mama's rocker. She must have loved rockers because she had three; one on the porch, one in the kitchen and one in the sitting room.

It was while occupying these chairs that Mama creamed butter and sugar with a big wooden spoon to create the world's best lemon loaf cake; told the children stories such as "Rapunzel" and "The Little Match Girls;" introduced us to Mark Twain by reading "Tom Sawyer;" worked her daily crossword puzzles, or worked on her current afghan. To Mama an afghan was a symbol, for as each of her children and later her grandchildren reached maturity, he or she was given one of her colorful handmade treasures. Each thought his the most beautiful, not necessarily because of the pattern or color, but because it was a personal gift of love made by Mama.

Few of us today truly know how to utilize our leisure. We rush around to plan vacations or take up a sport demanding an endless amount of equipment costing a small fortune, but even then we often fail to find the enjoyment we have anticipated. To fully appreciate our leisure time we should have learned from Mama. She and I shared many hours fishing from the boat dock at the Country Club lake. We both knew the only fish we would catch would be tiny little sun perch, much too small to put on a stringer, certainly too small to eat, nevertheless, we went fishing.

When she announced an upcoming fishing excursion, my life became filled with adventure and expectations. First, she had to arrange for someone to drive us; Mama never learned to drive a car. Then there was the afternoon we spent checking our fishing gear; two cane poles, a small tin of assorted hooks, a couple of spare corks and a stringer for our catch. The next day, we planned our lunch; should we pack sandwiches or cold fried chicken? Would we take bottled drinks, or would a jug of lemonade taste better? When the big day finally arrived, Poppa provided us with a coffee can full of worms, chauffeured us to the lake and wished his two fishermen good luck as he returned to his office.

I don't recall what we talked about on these very special days, but I do realize it was then my grandmother taught me to have patience, no easy accomplishment when dealing with a curious child.

At other times, Mama used her spare time reading. She read everything; tales of adventure, history, the latest novels, all the popular magazines like "Liberty" and "Collier's" and yes, even the latest trashy novel full of passion (as it was described by the social standards of the day) just to keep up with what the rest of the world was doing. When she read a risque book, she covered it with dust jacket from a less offensive one. Her little deception was never a secret, we all knew what she was reading; we also knew she didn't want us to know.

On rainy days, Mama amused her grandchildren by allowing us to build a blanket covered card table tent in the middle of the sitting room. We imagined journeys to the most remote parts of the world; deserts, jungles and rivers we had learned about from her. No matter where our pretended adventures took us, we knew we were safe because she was always nearby.

Mama taught me to enjoy moments of solitude, something few of us learn today in a world filled with so many electronic diversions. For all our one-on-one companionship, I am thankful; her time was so precious, yet she shared so much of it with me.

During the war her preparations for Christmas started even earlier as she made small fruit cakes and other delectable goodies. Everything you sent to servicemen overseas had to be packed in a regulation sized box. The tiny containers required more planning than one could imagine. Mama filled every precious inch with reminders of home, leaving no space to be wasted on packing paper. Small items were wrapped in a pair of warm woolen socks; envelopes of snapshots wedged between the carton and a tin of fruit cake cookies; packages of razor blades and pocket sized note pads were snuggled closely around a gift wrapped Zippo lighter; and handkerchiefs and boxer shorts were rolled so tightly they were unidentifiable. Each item was packed with all the love and attention she could muster and mailed early enough to arrive by Christmas. One year Mama asked me to get some music on the radio as she packed the boxes. While I'm sure she expected something like "Deep in the Heart of Texas" to be playing, I instead tuned in a station playing "I'll Be Home for Christmas," a melancholy song bemoaning the fact that a young man would be home if only in his dreams. Mama sniffed at first as a few tiny tears rolled down her cheeks. She put down her package, sat in her rocker and motioned for me to sit in her lap. We cried together. I knew as she held me that day, no matter how much she loved me, I was a substitute for the sons and grandson who were so very far away. We didn't talk; we just sat and rocked and cried and understood one another in a very special way we never shared again. It was one of the few times during the duration of the war I saw Mama cry. I never mentioned this to anyone else in the family; Mama wouldn't have wanted them to know she ever had a doubt in the world that all her beloved offspring would return home safely.

Christmas Eve was for the children. By five o'clock the entire tribe assembled for the most special of all children's nights. By six the dining table was set with delights served buffet style; there was sliced ham, fresh pork roast, gelatin salads shaped like Christmas trees, olives, pickles, cheeses and fresh fruit of every description. Even with such a mouth watering spread, this was the one night of the year I had no appetite; the anticipation of opening presents far out shadowed by desire for food. The women and children sat at colorfully decorated card tables scattered throughout the house, while the men relished a feast of fried oysters with all the trimmings served in the oversized breakfast room. The meal seemed to last for hours before the tables were cleared and put away. Once this task was done, it was finally time for the tree to yield its surprises for everyone.

Special chairs were moved from elsewhere in the house for my grandparents. After they were seated, everyone scrambled for a particular vantage point and the fun began. Poppa deliberated over who was to select the first gift before finally announcing his choice. It was the children's turn to add to the festivities; by then there were three of us–Bubba, George and me. Each of us worked diligently to learn some special skill for the occasion; playing a song on the piano, singing a Christmas carol or reciting a poem. Each had a turn. Before gifts were opened there were two more traditions; Poppa read the Christmas story from his well worn Bible and Mama played the piano as we all sang "Silent Night."

After those quiet moments to reflect on the true meaning of Christmas, bedlam prevailed. Squeals of joy burst forth from every corner of the room as we opened our gifts. The man got clothes. The ladies received blouses, cake dishes, figurines, handbags or other items of their dreams. In order to savor everyone's pleasure, Mama and Poppa waited until we had all opened our presents. Then, with the children sitting at their feet, they opened one gift at a time, taking time to express their gratitude for each before opening another. When all the hubbub died down, we knew it would soon be time to go our homes and to go quickly, for this was the night Santa Claus was to come. I never went to bed as willingly or as happy as I did on Christmas Eve.

The holidays during the war had some sad moments for our family. In 1944 Mama answered a knock at the door to find the florist delivering one red rose from Uncle

Ben when he was God only knew where in Europe. I got a Christmas card from Pud with a teary-eyed blue whale on it and a message to have a whale of a Christmas even though he could not be with us on Christmas Day. At that time Pud was somewhere in the Pacific so his mail carried a censor's stamp as did all the correspondence in those days. The war had even made Christmas different. What else was going to change?

Childhood memories of one's mother incorporate many, as many as there are individuals involved. To some Mother is remembered as the best cook in the world, to others as the selfless matriarchal thread who bound the family ties. If recollection of my Mother were pages in an album, each would represent her as a totally different person. She would be Florence Nightingale nursing Bubba and me through our childhood diseases; Scarlett O'Hara conniving to have things go her way; Emily Post expounding on good manners; Fannie Brice performing a brilliant comedy routine or Greta Garbo assuming the nonchalant posture of the most glamorous woman in the world. If these descriptions seem contradictory, then I've depicted my Mother perfectly. She was an experience, a medley of personalities that changed from moment to moment until she discovered the most appropriate for any given situation.

As the only daughter of grandparents' brood, she was spoiled not only by her parents, but also by her younger brothers. When she graduated from high school, Mother resolved to attend the Conservatory of Music in Cincinnati to study voice and drama. The fact enrollment there would take Mother over a thousand miles from home disturbed Mama greatly. The thought of sending a sixteen year old girl away to school was a foolhardy idea, especially sending her "up north." After intensified cajolery, Mother convinced her parents it was acceptable for her to go to Ohio. Stories of this monumental event were often related to me by both Mother and Mama, although their interpretations varied widely. Mama's most significant recollection of Mother's college days was the day she returned from her freshman year talking for all the world like a Yankee, an affectation totally unbecoming a proper young lady of the South. Mother on the other hand, loved to relive her experiences by sharing tales of adventure and snapshots with me. One photograph was of Mother, her roommate Willouise and a friend name Jane Froman was a strange sight indeed. The trio was standing in ankle deep snow, bundled up in coats with fluffy fur collars, while legs beneath their flapper length attire were protected by nothing more than sheer silk stockings. Mother had aspirations of becoming a famous singer; she studied music theory, counterpoint and harmonics, all of which she used lovingly as she sang lullabies to me and my brother. Her vocabulary was filled with such terms as "pathos," "empathy," and "passion," each as dramatic as her personality. It was a blend of these acquired theatrics skills and an innate sense of humor that placed Mother center stage among her family and friends. If she felt any misgivings about not pursuing a career in the arts, they were never verbalized; but, then they didn't have to be because I knew Mother was her happiest when she was entertaining.

In keeping with her flair for the dramatic, Mother often dressed in bright colors, crowning each ensemble with the latest hair fashion; a French twist, a Marcel wave, a pompadour or a shoulder length coif a la Southern belle. The times I remember Mother looking her most beautiful were when she and Daddy went to the annual President's Ball, to local social highlight of the year. This affair honored the President of the United States, Franklin Roosevelt. Unlike the current extravaganzas, however, the proceeds were contributed to research to cure a disease known as infantile paralysis. Mother would be more glamorous each year. One season she wore an emerald green satin gown that hugged her slender body in such a way she might have stepped straight from the pages of Harper's Bazaar. Her accessories were a rhinestone necklace and earrings, long gloves what went all the way to her elbows and a beaded evening bag that changed colors when I held it under the lights. On that night Mother was more gorgeous to me than the Queen of Sheba, Cleopatra and Norman Shearer all rolled into one. Because money was not plentiful there was no way Mother could top her costume with an evening wrap, such attire was a luxury few could afford in the 30's. To minimize the lack of such a garment, Mother draped her velvet collared Chesterfield coat over her squared shoulders, threw back her head and walked across the living room with the elegant air of royalty. I so wish we had owned a flash camera then so I could still enjoy seeing my parents all dressed up and smiling happily as they left for those parties.

Mother gave her best Oscar deserving performance when my brother was born. When she found out she was expecting (ladies were never referred to as pregnant), she threw a tantrum that lasted ever so long. I don't know if this was caused by the fact that finances were so short or not, but I suspect it was due to Mother's horror of gaining weight and partly due to the accepted and popular idea that mothers-to-be were to be pampered. Anticipated coddling offered Mother still another opportunity to upstage everyone else in the family, a position she relished with pride. On a cold November day, Daddy came to pick me up from school I knew something unusual had happened because Daddy never met me when school was out. As he opened the car door, he announced we were going to the hospital to see my new little brother. Having a baby brother was going to be great. Although my parents had talked about a baby, it wasn't until I saw him that I realized I'd no longer be the center of their attention. I was having second thoughts about a baby then.

Hospitals were open to children visitors so I was allowed to visit Mother and to hold the baby in my lap. One look at the fat little boy, no bigger than my baby doll, led me to smile and pronounce that he was my "Bubba," a moniker which has stuck with him to this day. When Mother came home from the hospital with Bubba she looked as pretty as she did going to a president's ball. She wore a bright red robe and had pulled her long black hair back in a bun. No matter what she wore I suspect the real reason she appeared so beautiful to me was that I had missed her terribly for the week she was away.

We lived in a small two bedroom Tudor style house; by today's standards it would be difficult for a family of four to have adequate room in such a dwelling. We had only two closets with the combined space of the smallest one in my current home, but there was no need for more. Daddy owned two suits, one for summer, the other for winter. The remainder of his wardrobe consisted of a couple of sports jackets and several pairs of trousers. Mother had several dresses for everyday and church, her annual formal attire, a suit or two and a winter coat. We didn't need much closet space. Although my closet was filled with Sunday school dresses, school dresses, raincoats and out of season clothes belonging to the four of us, it was never full. We filled our home with more important things like sharing and caring for one another and learning to respect each other's space as well as his possessions. Our house was always spotlessly clean. Mother had a real aversion to dust, dirt and disorder, even the hardwood floors were mopped every day after each piece of furniture had been dusted one more time. The organdy curtains were washed, starched and ironed so frequently they became threadbare before they were replaced.

When the ladies in the bridge club came to our house there was little preparation necessary; all Mother needed to do was make the salad or dessert she had chosen for refreshments. Her need for cleanliness didn't stop with the house by any means. Bubba and I were the cleanest kids in town. We sometimes wondered if Mother were going to leave us any skin as she scrubbed knees soiled by crawling in the dirt. When it was bath time, she opened the back door and called our names. If we didn't answer, she called louder the second time. The third time, she called us yelling out our full names. We knew for sure then Mother meant business and we'd scurry into the house on the double.

During the summer Mother bathed us before we took afternoon naps. Most children resist taking a nap, but not us. Mother's routine made nap time something to look forward to, for after each scrubbing we were rubbed with cooling alcohol as the gentle breeze of an oscillating fan swept across our weary little bodies lulling us to sleep. These naps were most important to Mother; rest was part of her plan to keep us from getting infantile paralysis, the most dreaded childhood disease in the world. The horrible crippler, later known as polio, struck children without warning, often leaving them lame or disfigured for life; in some cases even claiming their young lives. In the summer of 1943 paralysis ran rampant across the country as hundreds of cases were announced in newspapers. Schools in Houston postponed opening for a month because of an epidemic; almost a thousand cases were reported in Texas alone. We knew what to expect when Mother read of this situation. We were not allowed to go swimming, to play with kids who didn't live on our block or to go to our beloved Saturday afternoon movies. Since all these were perfect places for exposure to the malady, they were forbidden. I found it very inconsistent that even though we were not permitted to do any of the fun things, we were expected to go to Sunday School every Sunday. Was the church off limits to paralysis? If so, that's where I'd go if it ever got me.

Mother made sure Bubba and I had the grandest birthday parties ever. We had cakes with prizes baked inside. Whoever got the piece with the wishbone got a real prize, usually a coloring book, a book of paper dolls or a colorful sack of marbles. We invited our friends to wiener roasts, which were never complete without toasting marshmallows over the open fire until they dripped or fell from the coat hanger skewers into the flames. She and her friends dressed like gypsies and clowns to amuse our circus party guests. But, no matter what the party theme, there was always the birthday picture to be taken. Taking a snapshot doesn't sound important now, but it was extra special then. First everybody had to stand close together and face the sun, then Mother stepped back far enough to get everybody in the picture. Finally, after holding the bulky box camera at her belly button level for what seemed an eternity, she would push the button to expose the film.   Even her best efforts produced one of the world's finest collections of indistinguishable photographs of squint eyed, dressed up kids.

Our lives changed considerably in the winter. There was homework to be done, posters to be drawn for school projects and baths to be taken in a room steamed with the moisture evaporating from clean clothes Mother hung to dry. The first time I walked into a sauna, it was as though a time warp had returned me to our bathroom as it was when my brother was a baby. Mother kept the gas space heater turned up full blast all winter to dry Bubba's diapers. At times it was so hot it almost took my breath away, but it served its purpose well for my sibling always had dry, warm coverings awaiting his very frequent needs. I didn't see Daddy every day in the winter. It was dark when he left; I was usually asleep before he got home from work. Sometimes I wouldn't see him for almost a whole week. As the cold weather dragged on, Saturday became more and more important as the day I got to be with Daddy. Mother said she often felt like introducing my brother and me to him on the weekends. This problem solved itself as we grew older and the four of us enjoyed our evening meals together.

If ever there were undeniable proof that opposites attract it was Mother and Daddy. Daddy enjoyed being outdoors and camping; Mother felt that roughing it meant drinking an icy cold drink from a tin cup. Her only outdoor activity was swimming, a sport in which she excelled; Dad never learned to swim. Mother read every new novel she could acquire, assuming the air of its heroine until she finished the book; Daddy's reading was limited to the newspaper. He stayed cool headed in almost any situation rarely displaying a loss of control; she flew off the handle over any little displeasure. They never went on what one would call a real vacation because Daddy wanted to go somewhere he could relax and dress casually, while she dreamed of going to a big city, attending musicals and dressing up for a sumptuous dinner in the most elegant dinner club available. It wasn't their likes and dislikes I noticed as much as those things on which they agreed; their love for one another, and their children, their pride in their home, their devotion to family and friends and their mutual admiration for each other's sense of humor. Each enjoyed playing straight man for the other when amusing friends with outlandish stories and jokes.

Mother could impersonate almost anyone due to her dramatic training and a very good ear for speech mannerisms. Her skill at this added greatly to her stories as she adopted first the voice and manner of a British noblewoman, then the dialect of an Italian street peddler. On the occasions she used this talent, Daddy was her most appreciative audience.

Mother was always there for me whether she was serving as room mother to my class on Valentine's Day or nursing me through an illness. No matter what disaster befell my young life, she always made it better. To her, motherhood was a full time vocation; to me, she was an inspiration. I loved her dearly and knew with every ounce of being that she returned my love tenfold.

MY HEROES AND THE PRICE
THEY PAID

Soon after Pearl Harbor was attacked some of the local citizens were designated to serve on what was called a draft board. Shortly thereafter every young man in our town received a draft classification based on his age, marital status and line of work. One could tell when someone had been reclassified because of the serious family discussions following the arrival of that small piece of insignificant looking mail.

These tiny cards initiated changes that would influence my family for the rest of our lives. Uncle Collin was too old to be rated, but his son was not. The other men in our clan were classified and got their cards. Daddy and Uncle George were designated as 2A because they were married and the fathers of children. The remainder of my beloved uncles were listed as 1A. The arrival of a 1A draft notice impelled men to get their business in order quickly; they knew they would soon be in uniform serving their country.

Prior to the war there were few men from Crockett who made a career of, or even served in, the military. There was one young man who had become a career soldier. Colonel Edwin Ford had grown up a few blocks from my home, gone to military school, married his childhood sweetheart and attained the position of commander of an Army Air Corps base in San Antonio. Occasionally I'd see a sailor or soldier getting off the bus in front of the drug store when a local boy came home on leave, but these times were rare. In the city papers we got on December 7, 1941, there was the smiling picture of Lt. Robert English, another hometown boy who had just graduated from flight training at Kelly Airfield. Soon our small town weekly newspaper would report military achievements of most of the young men from the entire county.

Broadcasts of the news included accounts of long lines of men standing outside recruiting offices all night to enlist in the Army, Navy and Marines. Patriotism brought about some strange accounts as well, like the Rising Star Baptist Church in New Orleans changing its name to Pentecost Baptist to shed the name of the Japanese flag. Those who were Japanese , or even suspected of being so, were barred from all TWA flights. Many were moved to camps.

Zealous patriotic dedication was soon to effect our family as it did others from sea to shining sea. My two youngest uncles, Smith and Pud, went to Houston with a car load of Crockett men to enlist in the Army Air Corps. After they were accepted, the young patriots were instructed to return home until active duty orders were issued. Within a few days Pud was approached by the local Navy recruiter about enlisting in the Navy. Pud told the sailor he had already joined the Air Corps, not only because he wanted to be a pilot but also because he had no desire to wear bell bottomed pants. A short conversation convinced my uncle he could become a Navy pilot and get in the fight sooner. The next day on a trip to Dallas, he was accepted as a Naval pre-flight cadet, and sworn in along with 200 other young men on a broadcast on KRLD radio. He was told to go home and await his orders. Before his orders arrived, Smith's came. The two of them went to Mr. Reynolds' studio and had pictures taken to give Mama and Poppa. The family, although proud of them, regretted both would be leaving home possibly to face life and death conditions. In their customary manner, my grandparents took the experience in stride, repeatedly reassuring the rest of the family their offspring would be okay. It was as though they were trying to convince themselves of the same thing. For young men, one just out of high school, the other in his second year of college, it must have taken all the courage and guts they could muster to walk up to the recruiter and say "Take me." I'm sure neither had even the most remote idea what awaited them. It seemed so inconsistent to me, even then, that my mild mannered, easy going Uncle Pud was going into the full time business of killing people. In the war years paradox became the norm rather than the exception.

Smith on the other hand was the craftiest of the whole group. I never doubted he would return from the war okay, if for no other reason than I felt he would outsmart the enemy if necessary. I don't mean my other uncles were less intelligent, but Smith was very much more persuasive than his brothers. It worked for him too, for he managed to get based only 120 miles from home and was assigned as clerk to the base commander. He was put in charge of issuing supply requisitions, gasoline allowances, booze allotments and any number of other hard to obtain items. This clout gave the young man, hardly old enough to need a daily shave, the authority to finagle almost anything any GI wanted to do or to get. Soon he had most of the military personnel he worked with "beholden" to him. Thank goodness he stayed nearby; his frequent visits home were the only high spots in my grandparents' lives while their other sons and grandson were overseas.

Meanwhile, Pud, the most scholarly of the clan of uncles, sweated his way through basic training and pre-flight training in Athens, Georgia, ultimately completing flight school in Pensacola where he earned his wings. As fate would have it, he was assigned not as a Navy carrier pilot, but as a Marine pilot, which according to him was the elite of the Corps. He looked so handsome in his uniform when he came home on leave soon after earning his wings. Everyone was impressed with how manly and important he appeared in his dress whites before we all went to church together.

There may be Nobel Prize recipients, Olympic champions and Super Bowl winners who are proud of their awards but, never could there be anyone more proud than I was when Uncle Pud gave me his set of wings. He pinned them on my dress and told me to think of him every time I wore them. All the time he was away at war I wore those wings with the pride of a Medal of Honor hero. I was sure my pilot uncle would save us from those horrible Germans and dirty Japs who were trying to destroy the world. I use these descriptive terms for they were commonplace words by the time I got my wings. The propaganda machine in our country was working so well even Walt Disney cartoons had gotten into the act.

Children had become accustomed to referring to the Axis in such terms, even though most of us had little or no comprehension at all what made either of the Axis powers qualify for these dreadful designations. We knew for sure they were the enemies. Our loved ones were being killed, injured and kept away from us. That was enough to make the enemies unspeakable names in any child's mind.

Mama started a scrapbook which was to hold every newspaper article from our small local newspaper about the servicemen in our family. It was the custom of the armed forces to send photographs and accompanying mimeographed articles to each man's hometown paper proclaiming his latest contribution to the war effort, completing basic training, getting promoted, being wounded or receiving a medal.

Patriotism became a way of life, everybody of every did their part. Radio listing in the city papers carried the sponsor as well as the entertainment:

LADY ESTHER: Guy Lombardo Orchestra

GENERAL FOODS: Young Doctor Malone

WHEATIES: Jack Armstrong, the All American Boy

OVALTINE: Captain Midnight

Fifteen minute soap operas told stories of Ma Perkins, Young Widder Brown, Pepper Young's Family, Stella Dallas and Lorenzo Jones. Each night our radios were tuned to music by Harry James, Glenn Miller, Kay Kayser, Horace Heidt, Paul Whiteman, Tommy Dorsey, Fred Waring or Jimmy Dorsey. Fred Allen, Jack Benny and Amos and Andy amused us with their unique types of humor. These entertainments soon changed to encompass our need to buy war bonds, to save scrap metal and to donate blood. Broadcasts now resounded with reports from London by a young Edward R. Murrow and unforgettable songs like "Praise the Lord and Pass the Ammunition" and Kate Smith singing Irving Berlin's "God Bless America."

An overwhelming sense of pride became even more evident as small banners called service flags began to appear on the glass doors and living room windows of every house in town who had a family member away at war. At first Mama had a banner with two blue stars, one for Smith and one for Pud. Soon she purchased yet another flag, this time with three stars when Uncle Ben was drafted.

I've said little about Ben so far because he was the quiet one of the bunch, the brick, a more serious clone of Poppa. He was married by the time he went into the Army, but before marriage he had been the wild one; partying too much to make his grades at the University of Texas and having a ball wherever he went. He was not a bad young man, but he sure did enjoy himself. My grandfather put him to work after getting his grades from the University. When he returned home, he became known as one of the more dashing young bachelors in town; wearing his trademark felt hat tilted to the far right of his head of thick black hair made him even more alluring to the young ladies.

For all his cavorting prior to marriage, Ben became the most married of married men once he found Rebecca, the one girl perfectly suited for him. A few brief months after their marriage, Ben was drafted and his bride moved in to live with Mama and Poppa until his return. Since Aunt Rebecca was a teacher, I rode to school with her every morning. I soon learned to get dressed and ready for school early because we stopped at the post office to send a letter to Uncle Ben every single day. When he went overseas, the letters we mailed were much smaller and were call V mail, which meant Victory mail.

Ben endured the worst living conditions of all my servicemen kin. Even so, there was never a complaint from him, not because he found everything in the Army wonderful, but because he just did not complain. He was one of the thousands of men who hit the Normandy beaches on D Day. It was difficult for a youngster to understand what hitting the beaches meant. My only exposure to beaches had been having a picnic, building sand castles and getting sunburned. After seeing the gory newsreels, I realized the frightening agonies our servicemen were experiencing and it was indeed no picnic.

It must have been a particularly trying time for Ben, as it was for all those who were part of the greatest invasion in history, but for Ben it must have been more emotional because he knew the birth of his first child was imminent. I can relate to the despair he and Rebecca felt because when my first child was born, her father was somewhere in Korea with the First Marine Division. The insanity of war seems to pass from generation to generation in some part of the world just frequently enough to expose most of us to the idiocy of war. D Day was June 6, 1944; Ben III was born June 21st. It was late July before Ben knew he had a son.

When he finally got a well deserved leave from trudging the deadly battlefields of France, my Staff Sergeant uncle was sent to a famous ski resort for what he called R and R. I found out this was the Army's way of saying rest and relaxation. I got a letter from him telling me a gift was on is way, just for me. Awaiting this present filled weeks of my young live with anxious expectations. It arrived bearing a postmark I never deciphered and enclosed in a tiny box was small pin of crossed skis and a shield on which was printed a name I could not pronounce. That did not matter to me; what did was that even at war, my beloved uncle had thought of me. His thoughtfulness and his gift became equally as important as my wings. I wore them both every day and was the envy of all my friends at school. Each time someone noticed them I stood taller.

By now my cousin Collin, of bottle cap fame, had graduated from high school, entered the Air Corps and was stationed in England with the Eighth Air Force. He was even younger than Smith and Pud, so when he went away to war I knew the situation was really serious. He served as a radioman/gunner on one of the powerful B17 Flying Fortresses that bombed Germany's cities and factories until the madness in Europe was finally brought to an end. His plane was shot down but the Belgian underground troops got him and his crew back to England safely.

As more and more of the family became personally involved in the war, my grandmother's scrapbook grew thicker and thicker. In it were clippings about Smith being promoted to Corporal, and Sergeant and completing mechanics's school to service the new P38 fighter planes. The chronological articles regarding Pud included his completion of basic training, pre-flight school and of course, getting his wings. Along side these were pronouncements of his Distinguished Flying Cross award, Air Medals and his Purple heart and a letter that brought tears to my eyes each time I read Mama's book. It began, "The President of the United States of America regrets to informs you that your son Aldrich (Pud's real name) was wounded in action while encountering the enemy in the Pacific." Weeks went by before we knew if Pud was still alive, but Mama remained optimistic; the rest of the family was not so sure. When a letter from our hero finally arrived assuring us he was okay, there was not a dry eye among us even though Poppa did is best to conceal his tears from the rest of us.

Ben's representation in Mama's volume were stories of the usual basic training, reassignment and promotions from Private to Staff Sergeant in an antiaircraft artillery unit. Articles about D Day and awarded medals topped off the chronicles of Ben's military career.

On the pages of this journal were pictures of all our loved ones in their various military garb, fatigues, dress whites, leather flying suits and regular GI uniforms. One of Collin Jr. showed him nonchalantly leaning against the machine gun he manned on his B 17, another revealed Pud sitting in the cockpit of his Corsair fighter plane and there was a large picture of Ben being awarded a medal for bravery.

Intermixed with these were snapshots taken when our servicemen were home on leave, each one of which was crowded with as many of us who could get into the pictures. Others showed Bubba in his short pants saluting Pud, me wearing Smith's cap and several of Mama and Poppa with one of uniformed kin between them.

A section was devoted to Mama's grandson, Collin, even though his own mother, Dot, was faithfully preparing her own history of the war. On these pages were the usual accounts of basic training and promotions as well as Mama's version of the Belgium underground returning him to safety. The final, and most important entry of all, was the headline WAR IS OVER!

Not all the notations in the book had reference to the men in the family for there were reports praising Aunt Dot, Collin Jr.'s mother, for her devoted service to the local OPA (Office of Price Administration) rationing board, the success of the War Bond drive at the local movie theater and the achievements of the town's school children who collected tons and tons of scrap metal for the war effort.

While she was no historian in the purest sense, Mama surely had a sense of history, especially the history of our family. By the end of the war she had managed to record all that was important for our children and grandchildren to gaze upon at some point and feel the pride of the meager attempts, as well as the heroic feats, that held our family together like millions of others during the darkest days of our country's history.

THE WARS YEARS AT HOME

Milton wrote, "They also serve who only stand and wait." This statement was never more accurate than during the years of World War II. At the time of Pearl Harbor, all my uncles and Daddy were actively involved in the business of selling groceries for my grandfather's wholesale firm. As first one, then another left to fight the war, the burden of doubling up the work load fell upon the shoulders of Daddy, Uncle George and Uncle Collin. They were called upon to do the work four salesmen, two truck drivers and a warehouse supervisor had performed before the war. They did their part on the home front but were rarely afforded the luxury of either standing or waiting.

I've written of my war hero uncles but I've yet to recount the fondness I had for my other uncle. Collin, the eldest in the family, was a dashingly handsome man who had the keenest sense of humor of all my kin. He would tell the most elaborate shaggy dog stories imaginable, yet somehow get everyone to laugh at them. He delighted in pulling unique practical jokes on his friends and thereby became the envy of his cronies. He loved to fish with my Daddy, to play football with his son, to play poker with his friends and to dress like an English country squire in tweeds and expensive Irish wool plaid shirts ; but, most of all, he loved his wife Aunt Dot.

Without exception, Aunt Dot was the most thoughtful individual I've ever known. She was constantly doing little things for friends and family that endeared her to all. She maintained a complicated file of cards cataloging birthdays, anniversaries, graduation dates, weddings; every occasion one might have to celebrate. Although I never figured out how she did it, the mailman always delivered my birthday card from her on my big day. There were cards sent every day to Bubba when he had the measles or chicken pox, still others with puzzles I got when I had pneumonia. Her's was the first gift to arrive when a young couple announced an upcoming wedding or a new baby arrived. She had the capacity to comfort those who hurt, to laugh with those who were happy and to brighten the lives of all who knew her. She and Uncle Collin were very much a part of all Collin Jr.'s activities. They went swimming together, became active in the local Scouting organization as he won his various merit badges, suffered through all the sour notes as he learned to play the saxophone and attended every high school football game, even if he sat on the bench all night. The emptiness of their home once Collin Jr. entered the Army Air Corps prompted Aunt Dot to volunteer for a job on the local rationing board. She was perfectly suited for this job, for even though she was a very compassionate person, she was objective in her assessment of who really deserved coupons for automobile tires or other rationed items. Daddy said Aunt Dot was effective at saying "no" ten different ways.

When none of these methods worked, she turned on her charm or shamed people into admitting that doing without what they requested was a very small sacrifice compared to those of our fighting men. People who entered her office disgruntled often left feeling like true patriots.

For those who have never heard about a rationing board an explanation is due. We take for granted these days that if one has the money, he can buy anything his heart, his pocketbook and his credit card allows. This was most definitely not the case during the war. Everything, well almost everything, went into the combined effort of winning the war. Dresses got shorter to save fabric which could be used for uniforms. Little girls wore dresses made of printed flour sack their mothers had previously used for aprons, tablecloths and dish towels. Silk stockings and later nylon ones, became in such short supply women wore leg makeup and called it paint- on stockings. At Christmas, the traditional little red wagon boys got from Santa were made of wood instead of metal. Small inexpensive whistles marked "Made in Japan" were removed from the dime store counters and ceremoniously thrown into the local scrap metal collection to be made into bullets. While these shortages brought out the best in most Americans, there were those citizens who became known as hoarders, yet another word I had never heard before. These self-centered folks bought up tremendous amounts of everything they even remotely imagined might be limited for the duration. They had plans for either self indulgence or making big profits. For this reason, the government found it necessary to enforce a new set of strenuous restrictions on everyone.

Every man, woman and child was issued a ration book. Because I was not responsible for these books I never fully understood what all the requirements were, but according to Mother they were complicated. Periodically there was a ration book issued for every civilian. Apparently there were only certain periods of time one could use the ration coupons which were for specific types of merchandise. Some coupons limited the amount of sugar, coffee, and canned goods we were allowed; others restricted how many pairs of shoes we were permitted to purchase. Using these precious stamps was referred to as cashing points; once the due date was past they were totally useless.

Information regarding these stamps was highlighted in grocery store ads in the newspapers; brown stamps G, H, J, and K were good through December 4; green stamps A, B and C in Book 4 were valid through December 20th, etc.

In the name of patriotism we were called on to honor meatless Tuesdays when beef became scarce, and to grow victory gardens to produce enough vegetables and fruits in our own back yard to feed our families; fresh garden produce was not only more nutritious, but also freed up tin can metal to be used for much needed ammunition. As badly as Daddy disliked yard work, he planted a victory garden because it was his duty. I must say that for all his protestations regarding working in the dirt, Daddy had an excellent garden. I still remember the delicate flavor of vine ripened tomatoes, the crispness of the various greens and the delicious taste of just picked corn from Daddy's little farm. When we used canned goods there was yet another ceremony of patriotism to be followed. Mother cut both ends of the cans, removed the paper wrappers, washed the cylinders and put them aside until I took time to flatten them; even these mundane items were collected, ultimately to be shot at the horrible, dirty enemies of our freedom. Isn't it amazing, the flower children of the 60's want us to believe they invented recycyling?

Many people from small towns like Crockett moved to the cities during the war to work in defense plants. The ones in Fort Worth assembled airplanes; in Houston, they built ships. Women, who had preciously devoted their lives to being housewives, now worked on assembly lines producing everything from parachutes and uniforms to tanks, planes and weapons. Factories hummed with activity around the clock as workers created war supplies in three 8-hour shifts each day. Skilled workers were put to work immediately, others were trained at break neck speed. All across the country Americans had but one purpose: win the war and bring our loved ones home again.

In the forties almost all the GIs smoked, so cigarettes became hard to obtain. Daddy bought a funny looking hinged object used to make homemade cigarettes as uniform and tightly packed as the ready made brands. He taught me how to load the cigarette paper and loose tobacco in this gizmo while it was opened; when I shut the apparatus, out came a finished cigarette. I made Daddy several batches every week and carefully placed them in the empty cigarette packets he kept for that purpose. I don't know what happened to his cigarette machine after the war, but if I were to find such a gadget today, I'm sure I could still make it work. His fascinating pocket sized item afforded me an opportunity to help in yet another war effort.

When butter became a rare commodity, Mama placed a pound of shortening in one of her heavy ceramic mixing bowls and mixed a dark orange powder into it until it was the color of and consistency of butter. She called it oleomargarine. This was another new and strange sounding word to me. There were so many new words I often wondered if I'd be able to remember them as I grew older; words like barracks, Jeeps, atrocities, Quonset huts, flak, hoarders, slackers, kamikazes and saccharin. How in the world would I possibly store all this vocabulary in my brain?

As the war progressed and rationing continued, Mother took the only job she ever had outside our home. Just as Aunt Dot was issuing stamps, Mother was collecting them. Since our family was in the wholesale grocery business, it became increasingly important that the retail grocer turn in points in order to purchase more goods from wholesalers. Wholesalers in turn had to cash theirs with various suppliers so producers could get the governments' permission to buy commodities necessary to produce more goods. Everything got more and more complex, or at least it seemed that way to me. As the thousands of points came flowing into my grandfather's office, it became necessary for someone to collect them by classification and prepare them for the next step in the mandated process. Mother worked at this job every school day until I got out of school. Some days she would not complete the task before the end of the school day, so I often went to the office until she finished. Bubba was at home with Mama, so Mother's schedule could be as flexible as was required. Mother went about her duties with all the dedication of one in the more noble professions; it was her opportunity to make a personal contribution to our country's efforts.

As a rule when I went to the warehouse with Mother I would occupy my time working on my school lessons, climbing on the cases stacked in the warehouse until I could almost touch the huge rafters holding up its old gray tin roof, or standing in one of the open dock doors where boxcars were waiting to be unloaded. For some reason, however, one day I chose to stand in an empty doorway to watch a train go by.

A passing train was very ordinary but the train I saw that day was an exception. I had heard my parents discuss a camp which was being built about 40 miles south of Crockett; one to be filled with prisoners of war from Germany. The train I watched crawl through town that day was loaded with a cargo of those horrible Germans in route to the new camp. At first I was too terrified to wave back to the older, lonely looking men who waved to the little girl on the dock. A second look revealed men who looked very much like all the other men in my restricted world, except for their unusual haircuts. How could men with faces like these be trying to kill my Uncle Ben? They were the enemy! Why did they get to ride the train while my uncles were so far away and not allowed to come home? Why did they hate us? Why didn't they just go home and let things be the way they used to be?

Some of them didn't appear to be much older than my classmates. Were they allowed to come here with their fathers, or were the young ones really soldiers? The sight of these POWs was an experience I shall not forget, for each face reflected painful, aching loneliness and uncertainty. Later in my life, when my husband was away at war, I wondered if the children in Korea were as bewildered by our soldiers as I had been by the POWs I had seen so many years before.

As the train slowly dragged its caboose past the doorway, Uncle George came to tell me Mother was ready to go home. I ran into his arms crying that the Germans were here and were going to shoot us. I felt much safer after my handsome young uncle reassured me everything was going to be okay, that nobody, but nobody was going to get off the train and start shooting us. George was my uncle who could do anything, so if he said everything was okay, I believed him without question. He had very dark hair combed back with a thick coat of Vaseline hair tonic that made it shine like new patent leather. He had the dashing manner of the young Errol Flynn I had seen at the movies. When he and his wife Helen were first married, they lived with us until they could find an apartment. Money was not abundant in those days, so when something went wrong with the plumbing it was usually a financial disaster to Daddy. Daddy had many talents, but nowhere among them were the skills to make even the simplest types of repairs. When household repairs were necessary, George took charge. He could rewire lamps, fix the leaky faucet, paint the house, replace the arm on my injured doll and do any number of other things that somehow escaped Daddy's comprehension. Uncle George had an innate talent for handling animals, whether treating them for illnesses or injuries or training them to perform tricks. I often thought he would have been an excellent veterinarian, but then why stop at that, Uncle George could do everything.

He taught me how to ride a horse, how to feed a baby kitten found in a rainstorm, how to pick fresh berries, even how to fold paper airplanes that would fly longer than of any of my friends'. When Helen and George built a home two doors from use, I spent many hours with them. Aunt Helen, who had a naturally beautiful complexion, allowed me to use her rouge and face powder and taught me how to take it off with cleansing cream. After Little George was born, I often visited just to see the new baby. I was fascinated by my young aunt's ability to do all the things she did. She and Uncle George even made their own butter and cottage cheese, something I'd never seen done before. Although Helen was soft spoken and often appeared to be domineered by her husband's authoritative attitude, I soon learned she was much more in control of their household than I first perceived.

Back to our war efforts. At the same time food, shoes and metal were rationed, so was gasoline. Prior to the war one of the great pleasures our family shared was a Sunday afternoon drive. We watched Mr. Rutledge's cotton grow, oversaw every new section of brick being laid on the Murray house, noticed how much new wire Mr. Richards had stretched around his farm land and admired the new street signs our city had finally gotten installed. A regulation on the usage of gasoline quickly put a stop to these passive pleasures. Soon, everyone's vehicle had a strange sticker; a square indication of how much petroleum was allowed is driver. An A sticker designated the least amount, B was for those in the cities who needed gas to get to and from jobs essential to the war effort and C stickers were issued to the most critical automobiles, such as those belonging to doctors and trucking companies. Daddy was entitled to the least prestigious of these wartime status symbols. It took every precious gallon of gas he was allowed just to call on the customers he serviced in several counties. Our Sunday drives ceased. For a time, there was so little gas available, Daddy and Uncle Collin rode on the trucks taking orders for the next weeks supplies while the driver unloaded the shipment ordered the previous week.

Other shortages resulted in the necessity for scrap drives to collect metal, paper and rubber. We were called on to collect scrap rubber. Everyone expected to see a collection of old car tires and larger tires from trucks and tractors; few of us anticipated the weird collection of hot water bottles, boots, garden hoses and yes, even girdles and corsets, that appeared on the heap before it was hauled away for its vital purpose in a war plant. By this time, Mother had begun using lipsticks packaged in cardboard tubes because lipstick case manufacturers were now busy supplying casings for rifle ammunition. Crockett's largest war drive was one to collect metal. An announcement at school stated that every child would be awarded a certificate if he/she brought metal to our drive. Special recognition would be given to those who contributed the largest amount.

Families all over the county dug through tool sheds, garages, and barns for scrap; business cleared back rooms and warehouses of unused items. Tons and tons of metal accumulated on our school campus. This was my opportunity to make a difference; to help my uncles. After scouting the neighborhood asking for scrap, I became somewhat discouraged; many had already pledged their scrap to other students. I wanted so badly to collect enough to get the outstanding award, but seemed to be stymied. Where was I going to get enough to reach my goal? After weighing possibilities for ever so long, my solution occurred to me. I got credited for several hundred pounds of scrap Bud Rice hauled in from his farm. There were several wagons filled with old plows, bent wheel rims, rusty outdated farm implements and old horseshoes from my one source alone. I didn't get the special award, but I had done my duty to help in the war effort just like everyone else. That accomplishment was my award.

Still later there were paper drives. Newspapers, magazines and outdated files were tied in two foot bundles and deposited on the campus until it was hauled away to be reprocessed. Our magazines and books used smaller type and less spacious margins so that every word could be crammed onto as little paper as possible. Even letters to our loved ones overseas became measured, supposedly due to the amount of valuable cargo space they occupied on supply ships. This necessitated the invention of V mail,;

microfilmed copies of real correspondences. Magazines became increasingly important as a source of information about the war. Few of us will ever forget the memorable pictures of the walking wounded at Bataan, the sunken ships helplessly disabled at Pearl Harbor or the flag raising at Iwo Jima. All these historical events were captured by war correspondents and photographers and occupied their rightful places on the pages of LIFE. One who experienced those days is not likely to forget the famous "Four Freedoms" Norman Rockwell painted for covers of the Saturday Evening Post. They depicted ordinary American families in extraordinary circumstances caused by the war.

Joe Palooka, Terry and the Pirates, Snuffy Smith and Smilin' Jack all went to war in the funny papers. There were poignant stories written by a war correspondent named Ernie Pyle who reported the war not as an historian , but as an eyewitness of human reactions to the inhumane events the war spewed into our world. Bill Mauldin drew a cartoon about GI Joe. His skills pictured military life in such a way civilians could relate to Joe as one their own; lonely, caring; bone tired and ready to bring the horror of war to a close. Advertising changed as much as every other aspect of our lives. Lucky Strike green went to war when America's best selling cigarette changed the color of its package to white so the dye could be used for olive drab clothing and GI paint. We were encouraged to be patriotic by sneezing into Kleenex to prevent spreading colds that might keep war plant workers off the job. Grocery store ads included all current ration stamp information. At school we were reminded to urge our family to save waste kitchen fats to make explosives with slogans like "Your family's waste kitchen grease may gas an enemy plane." Posters appeared on our bulletin board urging us not to burn Christmas gift wrap but to save it for the next paper drive.

As I checked the newspaper each day for my next day's current events article report, I noticed how much more space was devoted to war news; everything from a front page story extolling the success of a tin can campaign in Houston, to accounts of the battles on the bloodied beaches of Pacific islands I'd never heard of before. Within days after Pearl Harbor, a new column appeared in every major newspaper; it was headed simply "War Casualties," and carried the name, rank, next of kin and hometown of those who had given their all for their country.
The lists grew longer, the type smaller in order to accommodate the ever increasing list of such tragic announcements.

In1943 the Allies had beaten the German and Italian forces in North Africa, then invaded Sicily. By late summer, the Italians surrendered unconditionally, but we still had a fight with the German troops who remained in Italy. In the Pacific we took Guadalcanal in the Solomon Islands but at a tremendous cost in the number of Americans we lost. Again, Movies mirrored our concerns when "Guadalcanal Diary," "Sahara," and "Watch on the Rhine" were made. With the end of the war drawing near, the U.S. Congress passed the GI Bill of Rights to finance college educations for millions of returning U.S. war veterans. The movies and the music took on a new air; lighter than before. There were movies like "National Velvet" and "Meet Me in St. Louis" that were set in quieter, more placid times than ours had been in the last few years. Phil Harris had a hit record, "That's What I Like About the South, " and folks were dancing to "Linda," "Sentimental Journey" and singing "Rum and Coca Cola" along with the Andrew Sisters.

June 6, 1944 was D Day. Front pages of all the papers proclaimed that church doors would be opened early for prayer. Whether by proclamation or by faith, Americans prayed that day; the churches were filled all across the country. City merchants bought full page ads which read, "The Time for Prayer is Here. Our Store is Closed Today," and "Our Invasion Day Prayer—May God be with Them, Please Let it be Short." Over 150,000 Allied troops landed on Omaha Beach and Utah Beach in one day. The surprised Germans had expected us to strike near Calais. We won the battles on those beaches but left a legacy of GI blood on sand as the casualties were tremendous.

Our British friends in the RAF dropped 2,300 tons of bombs on Berlin in one raid and U.S. bombers began daylight attacks all over Germany. Hitler retaliated with buzz bombs, called V2s. They had warheads of almost a ton each and took a heavy toll of almost 3,000 deaths and thousands of injuries. Even though we had taken the beaches on D Day, there were long and very costly battles that had to be fought. Gen. Patton led his tanks to the Seine in August and French troops liberated Paris later that month. In November President Roosevelt was reelected to an unprecedented fourth term as President and brought with him a new vice president, Harry Truman from Missouri. Things seemed to be moving at a quick pace and going well for the Allies until December when the Germans launched an offensive in the Ardennes Forest of Belgium. This pivotal conflict was called the Battle of the Bulge. Bad weather kept planes from air dropping badly needed supplies to the Allies. When German generals demanded our surrender, Gen. McAuliffe replied with a one word message, "Nuts!" Thankfully four days later the Third Army relieved the overwhelmingly outnumbered troops and the fighting ended.

In the Pacific U.S. forces took Saipan where over 30,000 Japanese fought to the death in a battle that lasted several weeks; it claimed over 3,000 Americans. In October, we regained control of the Philippines and Pacific campaign continued at a hectic and costly pace.

Radio programs listings were very important to us as we searched for the latest news from the fronts. Mother and Daddy sat by our console Philco every night to get the latest reports. Soap opera characters all had patriotic story lines added to their daily dramas. These shows were followed each afternoon by children's shows. Jack Armstrong; the All American Boy, Captain Midnight and the Green Hornet became preoccupied with uncovering spy rings; against these heroes, foreign agents had no chance of success. I couldn't wait to get home from school each day to hear how my idols had beaten the enemy spies one more time.

The most important of the daily radio shows were those of Murrow, Hottelet, Sevaried, Heatter, John Daly and Lowell Thomas with their reports of war news. The very voices of these dedicated men seemed to command attention, even from the most casual listeners. We were riveted into a state of somberness while listening to these programs. Radio patriotically participated in the war effort when Fibber Magee became a Civil Defense warden, Glenn Miller's orchestra played "American Patrol" and shows began with "Hello everybody, this is Bob coming to you from Camp Pendleton Hope," each from a different military base. Radio supplied most of America with a spirit which could only be communicated verbally, but more detailed information continued to be supplied by the printed media.

Songs popular during the war pulled at our emotions with everything from "Remember Pearl Harbor" to "Don't Sit Under the Apple Tree with Anyone Else but Me." Tunes like "The White Cliffs of Dover" and "Praise the Lord and Pass the Ammunition" were on the Hit Parade and the Jack Benny Show. At school we sang "God Bless America," "America I Love You," and "There's a Star Spangled Banner Waving Somewhere." Each song portrayed our love of country and our deepest desires to return to peace. Kids loved the satirical songs like "Wilberforce Get Off That Horse and Bring Him in for Lunch," which was introduced when meat rationing began and "Der Fuehrer's Face," in which one used the Bronx cheer to indicate what we would do to the heartless dictator. By now Little George was old enough to join Bubba and me in singing nonsense songs. His favorite was "Maizy Doats," while Bubba and I preferred "The Hut Sut Song." The mood of our family, as well as the rest of the country, was set to the beat furnished by radio; its character, molded by courage and faith.

Going to the movies remained the most popular form of entertainment; each film seemed to be designed to make us walk away more determined than ever to win the war. The newsreel reports showed our latest victories on both the European and Pacific fronts, but what I remember most about them is the weary, hollow-eyed, shocked expressions of the young men whose faces were shown. Walt Disney had Mickey Mouse and Donald Duck fight never-ending battles to slap the Japs and stamp out the Axis with all the talent he could muster. We watched "Thirty Seconds Over Tokyo," :"God is My Copilot," "Wake Island." and "They Were Expendable" with pride and admiration for the men who were protecting us so gallantly. A film called "Hitler's Children" aroused our indignation to point of hatred for those who were our enemies. "A Bell for Adano" highlighted the weariness our GIs were experiencing in their endless trudge back to the normal lives they had left so far behind them.

At the end of each movie, there was a short film clip made by Clark Gable, Robert Taylor, Robert Montgomery, James Stewart and countless others in the movie business who were now in the armed forces. Each related a story about the war with the skill only actors possess, but the ending was always the same, "Buy War Bonds." "Stamps are available in the lobby of this theater. Buy Your Share in American." Entertainers toured all over the country selling Bonds. Stars like Bette Davis, Greer Garson, Rita Hayworth and Betty Grable went to cities where they raised million of dollars through the sale of War Bonds. Less notable character actors toured smaller hamlets all over the country for the same purpose. It was a red-letter day when Franklin Pangburn came to Crockett for a War Bond campaign. Though he usually played the roles of priggish hotel desk clerks, he was a star of major magnitude in Crockett. He sold a record number of bonds to our citizenry. Even this aspect of the war was not without danger, for on one such fund raising trip the entertainment world lost Carole Lombard, a superstar of the day and wife of Clark Gable. We read stories of stars who traveled all over the world to entertain our fighting men with USO tours. One of these jaunts cost the life of famous big band leader Glenn Miller as he was in route to a base in Europe; still another condemned Mother's college friend ,Jane Froman, who had now become a star, to a wheelchair following a plane crash off the coast of Portugal. Everywhere they went the celebrities spread a dedicated spirit; the spirt of our country in a manner yet unmatched in our history.

Toward the end of the war I got a more personal lesson in the full meaning of patriotism when Daddy announced he had been reclassified as 1A. I understood what that meant; my Daddy was going to war.

Only one of my classmates had a father who had volunteered because, like Daddy, most of our dads had been rated 2A. The war must be getting even more serious than I thought, if my Daddy was being called; the Army just didn't take men with children. As my parents talked about what they needed to do before he went away the shock of the situation became more unbearable to me. I ran from the house and sat leaning against the back wall of the garage as I cried torrents of tears.   They simply could not take my Daddy away. What would we do without him? I don't recall how long I cried, nor do I remember what calming words Mother and Daddy said when they found me. For days I cried myself to sleep after praying to Almighty God that Daddy wouldn't have to go. I wasn't prepared to make this sacrifice for my country and if my reaction amounted to being selfish, that was okay with me. A turn in the war's progress made it unnecessary for him to go into the service, even though he was most willing to do so. When I heard this news I knew my prayers had been answered. Thank you God for listening to a little girl's plea.

Toward the end of World War II things were happening so quickly it was difficult to keep up with all the events, even though our teachers tried to keep us abreast of current events in most of our classes.

U.S. bombers raided Berlin at the same time the British bombed Dresden causing a disastrous firestorm. Our armored divisions reached the Rhine River and took over 300,000 German prisoners who were too tired and too out numbered to fight anymore.

There was a sense of optimism in the voices of my family as it became more apparent the end of the war was near. One Spring day in 1945, as I was busying myself by admiring the senior rings in Perdue's Jewelry window, a shocked man ran out of the barber shop next door shouting loudly, "The President is dead! Roosevelt is gone!" In an instant I ran to Mr. Carl's drug store where Mother was having a cherry Coke with a friend. Bewilderment was as obvious on their faces as it must have been on mine. Adults adapted to this shocking news much better than I. Mr. Roosevelt had been President of the United States all my life. I had heard so many speeches beginning with,"My fellow Americans," I could not envision anyone else being the leader of our country. The town, the state, the nation mourned the loss of our leader. Daddy, Poppa and the other grown ups discussed our destiny with a "haberdasher" at the helm of our ship of state. At the time, I did not know what a haberdasher was, but my family made it sound less than desirable. I could determine that much by the mere inflections in the voices of those I loved each time I heard them talk about the presidency. The serious confabs always ended with statements declaring that not even Truman could mess things up now; we were winning the war. Less than a month after Franklin Roosevelt died Berlin fell. Within days of FDR's death, Benito Mussolini, who led the Italian troops, was executed and his body was hung out on the street for all to see. The German armies still in Italy surrendered the very next day. Germany was defeated; they surrendered unconditionally; the madman and the madness had not prevailed. On May 7th VE Day (Victory in Europe) was proclaimed.

There was not the elation I had expected after such a long and bitter conflict; the battles were not yet over.

The Pacific front still stood between us and our dreams of peace. So it was that following VE Day everything remained relatively unchanged. Americans, civilian and military personnel alike, were still dedicated to ending the war with whatever contributions they could make. Day by day the war news got better; more optimistic. In the Pacific, we had rained incendiary bombs on Tokyo starting fires that killed half a million people. American troops took Iwo Jima after a month of fighting that cost the lives of nearly 6,000 U.S. servicemen and almost 20,000 Japanese. All these lives were lost for a island of less than eight square miles. After a three month battle, the U.S. secured Okinawa in June. This was another major gain for America; now we could execute air strikes against the mainland of Japan much easier than before.

The haberdasher had now been both accepted and respected as Commander-in-Chief by most of those who had doubted his effectiveness. In July our planes dropped leaflets on Japan. The message was clear, "Surrender or aerial destruction will be your fate."

Japan did not respond to these messages. In August, the leaflets were blunt and decidedly to the point, " Your city will be obliterated unless your government surrenders." Once again, the Japanese government failed to respond; they did not believe us. Truman courageously commanded the use of the first atomic bomb on Hiroshima. Over 100,000 Japanese citizens died immediately and nearly as many succumbed from radiation and burns later. Still they did not surrender. Three days later, a second A bomb named "Big Boy" was dropped on Nagasaki. This time over 70,000 people perished and an equal number died from the complications of radiation and burns. Finally, Japan asked for peace on August 11, 1945. In five short days the fighting stopped and the President proclaimed August 15th as VJ Day. Headlines all over the country carried the same words "WAR IS OVER." Again the newspapers were filled with ads as they had been on D Day, only this time they reflected the relief and great gratitude our country felt with messages which read "America is Grateful," "God Bless America," "Blessed Are the Peacemakers," "Thank God—It's Over," and "Victory and Peace—Thank God."

My friends and I decided to become a part of the celebration when events indicated the war was drawing to a close. We devised a plan we were sure nobody else could match. For days we worked making burlap bag effigies of Mussolini, Hitler and Tojo using old clothes we found in attics to dress them and painting pieces of cardboard with their evil faces. We were ready to let everybody know we too were glad the war was over. When the first bells rang and the local fire department sounded the siren, we knew our chance to participate had come. We saddled our horses and with all the pride of the Rough Riders dragged our childishly made effigies through the streets until we joined the celebration on the courthouse square. We continued to pull the Axis up and down the streets of our elated community until, at last, there was nothing left to drag behind our horses but the ropes with which we had tied them. God knows I was happy that day. I knew my uncles and my cousin would soon be home where they belonged.

This momentous day marked the end of time many would choose to forget, but I still remember vividly. Most children do not recall much of what happens in their early years, certainly I was no exception. I remember a few things prior to my sixth birthday, but not very much. For this reason the years from 1938 through 1945 were my childhood and most of that period was what my generation refers to as the War Years. If much of what I have recounted here seems to center around those dismal years, it is because that's what really happened.

You see, on August 6th the first atomic bomb was dropped; on the 8th, I celebrated my thirteenth birthday. The war was over and so was my cherished childhood.

Thank God, They're Home

As the servicemen returned there were almost as many adjustments to be made as there were during the war. I had expected them to come home tell grand stories of their brave exploits against the enemies; this rarely happened.

Ben had never seen his son, so when word arrived he was coming home, special plans were made for his arrival. Daddy was to meet his train in a nearby town and drive him home so Little Ben would not miss his afternoon nap. Rebecca changed clothes three times in preparation for his welcome before Mother convinced her that she looked lovely. When the car pulled into the driveway, Rebecca handed the baby to Mother and ran into Ben's open arms. Tears, smiles and kisses spoke louder than words as they embraced. As Daddy was getting Ben's duffel bag from the car, my uncle turned to Mother, took his baby boy from her arms and cradled his son in his arms for the very first time. It was a touching moment which became even more so when one of the insignia on Ben's uniform scratched the baby. Naturally the baby screamed and held out his tiny arms for his Mother as if to say, "Help me, I don't know who this is." Ben handed the baby to Rebecca and assured him everything was all right by saying " I understand son, I'll have to get used to you too.

Daddy turned away with tears in his eyes as we entered my grandparents' house. Every member of our clan took a turn hugging my uncle before we gathered in the sitting room for cake and coffee. During our visit I noticed Ben taking off all the paraphernalia he had been required to wear until at last there was nothing attached to his shirt but buttons. Only after this was done did he take his son in his arms once more. It was in this manner that Uncle Ben closed the door on his military life and opened a new one as he held his son in his arms.

After he was home for awhile, Ben told us he had been called the "Old Man" by the guys in his unit. The "Old Man" was in his late twenties and most of his buddies were either in their teens or very early twenties. The rest of the family found that amusing, but to me it seemed real; he had returned much older than the uncle I remembered before the War and I didn't understand why. One of his first priorities, after getting reacquainted with his wife and more comfortable with his son, was to buy a blue suit. He made it very clear that he had no desire to wear khaki, brown or olive drab for the rest of his life. He soon discovered this was not an easy mission to accomplish because every other veteran had the same desire. He became almost obsessed with the idea of owning a blue suit. He finally went to Houston in search of his wardrobe requirement returning only after he persuaded a clothier to recut a size 46 suit to fit his slender 36 long body. Once this was done, he began to act more like the uncle I had known in the prewar days.

The housing shortage that occurred across the country did not effect Ben and Rebecca. They found an apartment soon after his return and reestablished the marriage and home life that had been interrupted by his dutiful obligations. There were a few times he spoke of his experiences, mostly to make snide remarks about General Patton. According to Ben, his anti aircraft unit had softened up the front lines with days of bombardment before "Old Blood and Guts" Patton ever dreamed of taking tank units forward. He was bitter that Patton's outfit always got the glory and headlines while the artillery guys were just moved on to another clean up assignment. It was clear Ben could have cared less about headlines, but he could not pass up an opportunity to let whoever was listening know that the unheralded thousands like him had done more than their share. Soon, even those protestations stopped as he went about the business of getting his life back on track.

Smith's return to civilian life was seemingly easier than the others because he had spent the duration of the war on stateside bases. As a young bachelor, his first symbol of returning to civilian life was a new car. Since automobile factories had been converted to war plants, cars were even harder to obtain than blue suits. Nevertheless, Smith persevered until he was able to purchase a new Dodge coupe. With this accomplishment to his credit, Smith began to set the course for the rest of his life. It seemed out of character to me that Smith was dating. I couldn't remember him going out with many girls before he went to the Army. Once again, I had to accept the idea that the War had really changed my uncles.

Collin Jr. enrolled in the University of Texas shortly after his discharge, determined to be the first member of our family to get a college degree. Once in awhile he would speak affectionately about the people who risked their lives to get his crew back to England when they were shot down; on a few occasions, he told me about the peculiar way the British spoke the English language, but there was little conversation about his Air Corps life or his many missions over enemy targets in Europe. His silence indicated to all of us that he want to put his military life behind him and only look forward.

Of all my heroic kin, Pud's adjustment to civilian life was the most difficult. He had left home a handsome, innocent college boy; he returned a troubled, scarred veteran. When he was shot down over Okinawa the left side of his face had been blown apart. Gratefully the skill of Navy surgeons reconstructed his face, rebuilding his nose and part of his jaw bone with a new plastic material. The surgery left several very visible scars to remind him of his adversity. Through the years those scars faded and were hardly noticeable, but when he first returned home, they were protruded and discolored, looking like varicose veins over his eyebrow, under his eye and on his jaw midway between his chin and ear.

While it was shocking to see him so abused, the scars weren't as unsightly to the family as they must have been to him. He held a handkerchief over the left side of his face even when he was eating and sat with his left side turned to the wall whenever possible. He and Jane got married shortly after his return, but he would allow no one to attend the wedding except her maid-of-honor and his best man, a fellow Marine pilot. Although it was against his wishes, the families were permitted to have a small reception after the simple wedding ceremony at

Brother Lee's home. His one stipulation however ,was that no pictures be taken.

For months Pud had recurring nightmares and even though he was sent to Pensacola for several months to train new pilots, it was long after his discharge before the horror of War began to release its grip on him. Years later, he related to me what had weighed so heavily on his compassionate spirit. His experiences encompassed the dismay of landing next to his wing mate's crashed plane to see his buddy trapped and burning to death under his Corsair's fuselage. Pud was powerless to save his friend; a burden he would carry throughout life. Later, just before he was to leave for the Pacific campaign, he was ordered to fly some test missions over a desert area somewhere in Utah. He was told the tests were deadly gas bombs which could hasten the end of the war and was given specific instructions to be very careful to fly into the wind when he dropped them; otherwise, the gas would be fatal to him.

A few days later he was shown photographs of prairie dogs from the test area; swollen to the size of hogs before effects of the lethal gas finally caused their bodies to burst. He questioned the necessity of such warfare; it caused him to wake at night screaming. He could not use such an implement of death on another human being, enemy or no enemy.

After he got into the thick of the Pacific battles, he flew under the wing of a squadron member for 2 ½ hours guiding his fellow Marine back to the base after his buddy's left eye had been shot out. On occasion, Pud mentioned a Japanese bombing raid that to him exemplified abject terror. He and another pilot had jumped in a South Pacific bunker during the attack. According to Pud's account of this event, he drank a full bottle of bourbon in a few short minutes but was so frightened, empty bottle and all, he emerged stone sober. Surely not all his war scars could be concealed by his handkerchief, yet his compassion never failed. He was still the gentle, caring Pud who years later upon locating the grave of a Marine side kick in Hawaii, knelt, patted the grave and said affectionately, "So long, buddy. I'm glad I finally found you."

The War changed all my loved ones, as it did millions of others, but at least they came home. Colonel Ford did not, nor did Lt. English, the hometown boy whose picture was in the paper on Pearl Harbor Sunday. Mrs. Robinson and Mrs. Fulgham hung gold star banners in their windows when they lost their sons Hop and Pat. Slugger McGraw returned with one leg, never to play football again. Frank Shanks had been in a German prison camp and even though he had been in an Army hospital for months before he came home, still looked like a walking skeleton. His three brothers all came home safely. The Welches welcomed their three sons and one daughter who had served their country. Our neighbor Vira cried buckets of tears of joy when her three younger brothers returned. Jack Beasley Jr., Rollie Traylor, Dan Julian, Lyle Thomasson, and Carl Murray all came home from the U.S.Navy. Herbert Callaway came home from the Army with citations and medals for every battle he fought in Europe. Countless men returned from the

Air Corps without a scratch. Some were not that lucky; they bore scars from horrible injuries; others weren't so visible. Many returned as heroes. Mutt Knox won the Bronze Star while serving as a Marine Corps Captain; Roy Garner had a chest full of medals beneath his Navy wings; Douglas Arnold matched these heroic feats with his tour of flying the "Hump," the name given the Himalayas by the pilots in that theater of war. Jake Caprielian enrolled in the University in Austin grateful he would never set a bomb sight again.

One by one, they were discharged from the various branches of the military. There were no parades proclaiming their return, just happy families reunited after painful separations. They picked up the pieces of their shattered lives to become mailmen, merchants, manufacturers, craftsmen, salesmen, teachers, farmers, bankers, attorneys, ranchers, business men and doctors; all dedicated to the common purpose of living peacefully for the rest of their lives.

The first Christmas Eve they were all back home was very special. Poppa said a longer than usual prayer thanking God for everyone's safe return and the many gifts He had bestowed on us. I can't remember any of the gifts we opened that night; they really weren't important. What was important was that we were all together again and I felt safe again in the bosom of my family.

About The Author

Carol Dickey Watson worked as a reporter, copywriter and public relations representative after graduating from Southern Methodist University in Dallas with a degree in English. The single mother of two daughters changed her career path in pursuit of more lucrative employment in retail management for Sears, Roebuck and Co. and Federated Department Stores until retirement in 1988. Her first love was always writing but since she had two precious girls to rear and to educate, a career in writing would not always pay the bills, much less educate Donna and Marti. She started this book in 1960 and has finally finished it 46 years later. Her life has been filled with the joys of having her daughters, their four active sons and a great grandson become the center of her world. It was for these important individuals that the book was written so they might know what life was like for a young girl growing up during the dreadful years of World War II. Thankfully her family did not experience the tragic losses of many families, but the changes that occurred during the War left lasting impressions on the girl who was only nine when Pearl Harbor was attacked.

Printed in the United States
76507LV00001B/253-498

9 781425 962081